BACKPACKER
THE OUTDOORS AT YOUR DOORSTEP

Hiking Light Handbook

BACKPACKER
THE OUTDOORS AT YOUR DOORSTEP

Hiking Light Handbook

**CARRY
LESS
ENJOY
MORE**

Karen Berger

THE MOUNTAINEERS BOOKS

THE MOUNTAINEERS BOOKS
is the nonprofit publishing arm of The Mountaineers Club, an organization founded in 1906 and dedicated to the exploration, preservation, and enjoyment of outdoor and wilderness areas.

1001 SW Klickitat Way, Suite 201, Seattle, WA 98134

BACKPACKER
THE OUTDOORS AT YOUR DOORSTEP
33 East Minor Street
Emmaus, PA 18098

Published simultaneously in Great Britain by Cordee, 3a DeMontfort Street, Leicester, England, LE1 7HD

Manufactured in the United States of America

Acquiring Editor: Cassandra Conyers
Project Editor: Kate Rogers
Copyeditor: Joan Gregory
Cover and Book Design: The Mountaineers Books
Layout: Mayumi Thompson

Unless otherwise noted, all photographs are by Karen Berger and Daniel R. Smith

Cover photograph: *Hiker Crosing Creek in Evolution Basin, John Muir Wilderness, Sierra Nevada.* PatitucciPhoto©
Frontispiece: *View down Goat Creek Valley, Mount Adams.* Photo by Alan Bauer.

A cataloging-in-publication record for this book is on file at the Library of Congress.

♻ Printed on recycled paper

Contents

Chapter 9

Walking the Walk: Footwear   **143**

Introduction:

Carry Less, Enjoy More

O ver the past fifteen years, "lightweight backpacking" has become one of the biggest trends ever to hit a hiking trail. You cannot go into retail store, read an outdoor magazine, or strike up a gear conversation with a serious hiker without the word "ultralight" creeping in somewhere.

Not convinced? Then follow the money and take a look at what manufacturers are calling their gear. Terms such as microlite, gossamer, and ultralight abound, as do names intended to conjure images of lightweight comfort: "the cloud," "the ghost," "the feather," "the breeze."

The reason is simple. Anyone who has ever planted boot to trail has at some point carried too much weight. Every one of us has returned home from a hike with the realization that we not only packed twice the gear we needed, but that we also carried it every step of the way. We have all wondered whether we could lighten our loads.

The answer is a resounding "Yes."

An overweight pack causes our necks and shoulders to ache. It slows us down. It makes us breathe more heavily going uphill and step more heavily going down. It puts pressure on our knees and ankles and increases the chance of injury. An overweight pack just plain hurts, compromising our enjoyment of our trip. It takes only a mile or two under a too-heavy pack to start appreciating the old saying "Less is more."

Most likely, that's why you picked up this book.

Perhaps you've been on a trail with aching neck and knees, wondering just how you were going to make yourself pick up that behemoth pack one more time—let alone actually carry it somewhere. Perhaps you've seen hikers with lightweight packs striding easily past you, and you wondered whether it was really possible to camp safely and comfortably with only half the stuff in your pack. Were the lightweight

Opposite: Sage overlooking desert lake. (photo by Alan Bauer)

hikers as crazy as they seemed? Or did they know something you didn't? Or maybe you've seen advertisements for new lightweight gear making seductive but seemingly impossible promises: a pack that weighs less than two pounds, a shelter for less than a pound, clothing that weighs only a couple of ounces.

Indeed, sometimes the idea of lightweight backpacking (not to mention the claims of lightweight backpackers) does seem too good to be true. As lightweight backpacking has moved through the backpacking community and the outdoor equipment industry, it has attracted converts and proselytizers, dreamers and innovators, along with a handful of iconoclasts and rebels. It has also polarized hikers. Extremists float along under gossamer packs, flouting the laws of nature with barely more than a tissue for a tent and three granola bars for dinner. Meanwhile, traditionalists cling to their heavy loads in the name of comfort and safety, consoling themselves that should a hurricane, an avalanche, and a flood all strike at once, they are prepared for all three, and can whip up a gourmet meal to boot. Each group thinks you should do it their way.

Then throw the manufacturers into the fray. You'll find small-scale mom-and-pop innovators making hand-sewn tents and customized gear with the goal of sharing strategies they've developed on trails. More ambitious hikers-turned-business people have applied bonafide MBA-skills to lightweight backpacking products; the results gleam with finely honed marketing sheen. Traditional manufacturers have gotten into the act, borrowing, modifying, and (occasionally) co-opting lightweight designs, bringing them to the mass market.

Add to that the confusion of too much advice: Ask three experienced hikers about the contents of their packs, and you'll get three different answers. Ask another ten, and you'll get ten more. One writer on the subject claims that using a tightly cinched hip belt limits freedom of motion; another states unequivocally that pack weight should be placed on the hips and the belt tightened as much as possible. One expert advises never to skimp on food; another is experiment-

Not a lightweight pack! The author tries on a porter's load in Nepal.

ing with fasting on the trail. I've had people tell me that an umbrella is the single most indispensable piece of gear they carry—and I've heard other people say it's the single most useless. Who's right? Who knows?

Too many choices, too much conflicting information. If you feel as confused as a hiker in a thick fog at midnight, you're not alone.

This book can help.

But first, a disclaimer.

This book will not teach you to backpack with less than ten pounds on your back.

It will not teach you to hike 35 miles in a day.

It will not tell you to leave behind your sleeping pad, your cookstove, or your shelter.

It will not tell you that fasting while backpacking is an opportunity to save on food weight and lose body weight at the same time.

It will not suggest that you hike barefoot.

All of these suggestions have been made by writers and speakers on the subject. Indeed, some highly skilled, experienced, and ambitious hikers have hiked with loads weighing less than ten pounds, or have covered 35 or 40 miles a day, or have hiked long distances barefoot. These kinds of feats tend to garner a lot of attention, both among hikers and sometimes in the media, but such feats represent only a small part of lightweight hiking. For the most part, lightweight hikers carry more than ten pounds; hike fewer than 35 miles a day; take along sleeping pads, stoves, and shelters; eat food; and wear boots.

We can learn a lot from lightweight hiking innovators and those at the extreme end of the ultralight spectrum. I for one stand in awe of their achievements. But let's be honest: Most of us don't want to hike 40 miles a day, or live through a blizzard in a tarp, and most of us want one or two creature comforts. Applying what these hikers do for an everyday hike may work for some of us—but not all. Most of the lightweight material currently available assumes that hikers want to hike long miles, or share the author's passion for absolute minimum ultralight loads. My experience has been that while long-distance and average-distance hikers can benefit tremendously from lightweight and ultralight techniques, most hikers—regardless of distance—are not necessarily interested in being total minimalists. Rather, they are looking for ways to minimize pack loads without feeling that they've gone beyond their comfort or safety margins.

This book will give you the suggestions for getting started on the lightweight path. It will discuss one-pound packs and stoves that weigh an ounce and lightweight tarps and sleeping coverlets. If you are interested in serious information about ultralight hiking, you'll find plenty of ideas. But ultimate mileage and skating on the edge of safety is not this book's goal. Rather, this book is intended for the vast majority of hikers who want to be comfortable and safe in the wilderness—with the minimum load that will allow them to have a good time as they define it. If you've already got your base pack weight down to ultralight standards, this book won't tell you where to shave off those last two ounces. If you have pared down your gear so thoroughly that the only way you can save another ounce of weight is to leave your food at home, you are way beyond the information you'll find here.

But if you've been suffering under the load of traditional gear, or if you've "hit the wall" and can't figure out how to lighten your load even though you commonly see other hikers carrying less, this book will give you some strategies and solutions that will help you hike safely and sanely with less on your back, whether for a weekend or a multi-month thru-hike.

While I'm on the subject of caveats, I should also mention that I'm not going to give you a single ironclad prescription for success. Yes, a lighter pack is more comfortable than a heavier pack. And yes, this book is stuffed with ways to make that lighter pack a reality. But it's also stuffed with choices that you will have to make. The way I see it, my job is to describe these choices and their ramifications, and to talk about when they tend to work best and when they don't work at all. It's my job to give you strategies and warnings, and to help you think through the many options available. It's your job to apply this information to your hiking style, your mileage, and your environment. Think of this book as a road map—with you in the driver's seat.

During the course of hiking America's Triple Crown Trails, along with many other long-distance trails worldwide, I've seen hikers experiment with hundreds of different weight-saving strategies, right down to the old cliche of sawing off a toothbrush handle. I've seen hikers modify their gear as they learned lessons from the trail about what they needed and what they didn't. I've seen hikers trade heavy packs for light packs—and I've seen hikers trade light packs for heavy ones. I once watched an overburdened backpacker happily haul a seventy-pound pack into the woods—and then come back for a wheelbarrow filled with a cooking grill and a cooler full of steaks. Not something I would do, but he seemed to be having a good time.

Mostly, I've watched people learn, and I've learned from them. I've seen hikers adapt to a variety of conditions, I've seen hikers change their gear as their needs changed and their skills improved. I have seen hikers start with one philosophy and shed it as they interacted with the environment. I've learned from their mistakes, and I've learned from my own.

In this book, I share that knowledge, and hope that the result, for you, will be a safe hike with a light pack.

How This Book Is Organized

This book begins with two chapters discussing some of the broader issues of lightweight backpacking. What exactly do we mean by lightweight backpacking, and who is well-suited to lightweight techniques? How is the lightweight mindset different from the traditional mindset? What general strategies apply? What trade-offs do lightweight hikers make? What risks do they take? These chapters are designed to give you a framework for thinking about lightweight backpacking strategies and issues so that you are better prepared to evaluate each piece of gear within the context of lightweight strategies.

Chapters 3 through 9 discuss gear. Each chapter discusses the function of a category of equipment, the traditional gear choices commonly available, and lightweight alternatives. I also discuss strategies and techniques for reducing weight and for getting the most out of your lightweight gear. For example, the tent chapter (Chapter 3) discusses how selecting an appropriate campsite can enable you to use a lightweight shelter such as a tarp without sacrificing comfort or safety.

I haven't loaded the text with recommendations for specific types of gear. One of the great frustrations about writing about gear these days is that styles and models are brought to market and then put out to pasture in the blink of an eye. Many of today's hot-selling light-

Hiking light makes climbing over stiles a breeze.

weight items will be replaced by new models and designs by the time this book reaches a bookstore. Some of these new styles, undoubtedly, will be lighter than what is available as I write this today. And some will be heavier. So instead of focusing on particular models, I've provided information that should help you evaluate various kinds of gear, no matter how much the designs change from one year to another.

Nonetheless, sometimes I have found it useful to use particular kinds of equipment as examples and illustrations of how certain styles of products, materials, and designs solve backpacking challenges in a lightweight manner. The Z-Zip wood-burning stove, for example, is just about the only wood-burning stove that has been consistently on the market for many years. Similarly, the gear company GoLite specializes in lightweight backpacking equipment, some of it modeled after the ideas and designs of lightweight backpacking innovator Ray Jardine. Not to mention such a resource would be unhelpful. Sometimes, a particular model of gear solves lightweight backpacking problems in a unique way, and I decided it would better serve the reader's needs for me to call attention to such a product rather than to be vague about it.

I have reluctantly decided not to describe by name the many excellent and innovative products produced by small, independent mom-and-pop companies. While researching this book, I found too often that a promising company from which I collected information as few as six months previous is now out of business. These companies, being smaller and design-driven, also tend to change their products faster than a writer can keep up with them. In some cases, I've been told that models available for sale today are being replaced by new and improved models whose design specs are not yet available. This is especially true with companies doing most of their business over the Internet. I encourage you to use the Internet (search "lightweight hiking" or "lightweight backpacking" and you'll get a gaggle of hits) to find currently operating companies and new designs; you'll find a lot of intriguing ideas, and quite possibly, some great lightweight gear. Also refer to Resources, at the back of this book, where I list some of the most useful Internet sites (although please be aware that websites change with time or go out of business altogether).

You'll probably be quick to notice that I've left discussions of backpacks and boots to the very end of the book. At first glance, this might seem odd. After all, boots and backpacks are the two items that offer the biggest potential weight savings, and most authors who tackle the subject of lightweight backpacking put them right up front, perhaps to display the pounds that can be shed so easily with one fell swoop.

This is one issue on which I differ

Two packs, a hiker, and a Scottish bothie. Which load would you rather carry in the morning?

from many other writers on this subject. The reason is simply this: I have seen far too many hikers cut back on their packs and their boots before they cut back on the weight they are carrying. The result is all too common: The load is too heavy for the gear designed to carry it, and the hiker suffers pain in the back, neck, shoulders, and feet.

Think of it this way: Would you rent a moving van before you knew how much stuff you planned to move? Would you buy a suitcase before you knew how long you were traveling and how much stuff you needed to take? Then why would you consider backpacks and boots—whose job is, after all, to help carry your gear—before you knew how much gear you were going to carry?

Heavy boots and packs are designed to carry heavy loads. To do this, they use features that weigh more, such as thick leather uppers on boots, and big hip belts and suspension systems on packs. Boots and backpacks do yield the biggest weight savings—but only after you've done the work to get the rest of your gear into shape. That's why I talk about them last.

By the time you get to the point where you can slip on a pair of lightweight trekking sandals to shoulder your newly svelte lightweight load, you'll have developed a system that works for you—comfortably, safely, and sanely. Enjoy!

Chapter 1

Thinking Your Way to a Lighter Pack

The idea of lightweight backpacking is not new. Backpackers have been experimenting with lightweight strategies for years. In the 1984 edition of his classic, *The Complete Walker,* Colin Fletcher pointed out, "It presently seems to me—and to many others I have consulted—that if you never attempt weekends in more than smiling or familiar country and hug frequented trails or always have companions to bail you out of trouble, then equipment failure due to marginal reserve strength or the lack of a nail may be a mere nuisance, a risk well worth taking; and if you so choose you can safely and advantageously ride the New Wave. But if you know you may find yourself alone in a mountain storm, three days from roadhead, then false weight-economy could prove fatal; and you had better forget the gossamer game . . . "

Gear has changed in the years since that penultimate edition, and today's gossamer fabrics and high-tech components are often as sturdy as their traditional counterparts. But the debate about lightweight hiking and safety still rages among hikers.

What is new is that lightweight techniques have finally spread into the mainstream. The trend gained momentum on long-distance trails, where pack weight

Opposite: Admiring a trailside cedar tree. (photo by Alan Bauer)

and mileage are both constant topics of discussion. Ray Jardine's seminal *Pacific Crest Trail Hikers' Handbook* showed how lightweight strategies could help hikers, among other things, achieve the high daily mileage needed to complete a single-season thru-hike of the PCT. Other hikers took notice, understanding that long-distance hikers were learning something that was well worth watching. Some manufacturers resisted the trend, arguing in favor of durability and the safety of traditional equipment. Other manufacturers jumped on what they saw as an obvious and appealing bandwagon: lightweight backcountry comfort. The marketplace voted; the verdict is split. Both traditional and lightweight styles have their fans. But as lightweight gear goes mainstream, hikers are learning that they can trek as safely with a lighter load as they could with a heavier load. More and more are going into what Fletcher called the "gossamer game."

Indeed, today it sometimes seems that the terms "lightweight" and "ultralight" are ubiquitous in gear catalogs, in magazine articles, and on Internet sites. However, as we'll learn as we discuss each piece of gear, calling something "lightweight" doesn't necessarily make it so. New designs, new high-tech materials, and new marketing trends have all changed the playing field of outdoor retailing in the last few years, and the result is a confusion of products addressing trends in the market place. Those trends include, in addition to lightweight hiking, extreme sports, short-duration intense trips, and "skill" sports such as rock climbing and kayaking. For the backpacker looking for lightweight functional gear, the maze of choices can seem overwhelming, and the fact is that product labels are not always helpful, or even accurate. When you see a seven-pound tent advertised as "lightweight," you know that the message is being mangled somewhere along the pipeline. Your defense: Clear knowledge about the need each piece of gear must address, and an awareness of how little a piece of gear can and should weigh.

Lightweight State of Mind

Lightweight hiking and traditional backpacking both have parallels in mountaineering. You may have read stories about some of the early mountaineering expeditions to major Himalayan peaks, involving a team of climbers and a virtual army of Sherpas. This siege mentality assumed that high mountains were places where people couldn't survive for long without being fully equipped and prepared to withstand anything the mountain might throw at them. The mountaineers would stick out whatever happened with the help of tons—literally—of supplies; they would essentially lay siege to the mountain. These siege-style mountaineers are akin to traditional backpackers: Fully equipped and heavily laden, they are ready for the worst.

In contrast, the newer, hipper, alpine-style climbers are light and fast. They don't argue that high mountains are dangerous places. But instead of laying siege to the mountain, they rely on being fast and light enough to summit and descend

A well-packed, traditional load shouldn't weigh more than 20 or 25 pounds in three-season mountain conditions.

before the mountain figures out how to thwart them. Alpine climbers pick their time. They are akin to lightweight hikers: Fast, light, skilled, ready to change their plans at a moment's notice, and well aware of the risks they are taking by traveling without a safety net.

And, to carry the comparison one step further: Ultralight hikers may be the equivalent of the extreme alpinist who travels solo without oxygen.

Both the siege style and the alpine style of mountaineering succeed in putting people on summits. Same with backpacking: People have hiked long trails successfully with mammoth packs and with lightweight packs. So it's not a question of what works. Both styles clearly do. It's a question of what works for *you*.

Different Hiking Styles

How lightly you choose to travel is a personal decision that will reflect your personality, goals, comfort level, and experience. The heavyweight traditionalist and the ultralight extremist are on either end of a spectrum, and as you read through this book, you'll make choices that will move you from the heavy end toward the light end. Or you may choose to stop somewhere in between. Most experienced hikers find themselves happy, safe, and comfortable somewhere in the middle of the lightweight category. Look at the three categories below and decide which one best describes your hiking style.

Traditionalist

Some hikers want a more comfortable pack, but they don't want to change their hiking styles. These hikers can move easily from a heavy load to a lighter, but still traditional, one simply by losing some excess weight—by trading in a seven-pound tent for a four-pound tent, for example, or by exchanging heavy leather boots for lightweight hybrids. They're not doing without or changing their essential gear list. They are merely replacing heavy gear with lightweight alternatives that do the same job. Granted, they might give up a few options: The new lightweight tent may not have as many gear-storage pouches or as much headroom, or the new pack might be short on extra pockets. But they are still carrying the same basic equipment, with no concern about compromising comfort or safety.

Open-Minded Experimenter

Farther along the continuum are hikers who want to make real changes in their hiking styles. Commonly, such hikers are also interested in maximizing trail mileage. Since they intend to spend most of their waking hours walking, they are not as concerned with in-camp comforts, such as a tent big enough to play a hand of cards in if it's raining. They're not spending their afternoons casting for trout, so they don't need a pan big enough for frying fish. And for them, camp shoes are a ridiculous luxury: First of all, these hikers are already wearing lightweight shoes, and secondly, they're not spending enough time in camp to be bothered with evening footwear. Lightweight hikers are willing to experiment with their preconceived notions about what they actually need to take on the trail—even if such experiments occasionally compromise their comfort. They are willing to explore new kinds of gear: Can a tarp really protect someone in a rainstorm? Do the new alternatives to traditional (and heavy) waterproof-breathable rain suits work? Can you really swap a full-featured traditional backpack for an unframed rucksack and not have aching shoulders at the end of the day? Hikers who are willing to experiment open-mindedly with these issues have moved out of the traditional camp into the lightweight camp.

Risk-Taking Innovator

Way over at the ultralight end of the spectrum are folks for whom an ultralight pack is the ultimate priority. The ultralight hiker is ruthless about what goes into his or her pack, concerned first and foremost with the relationship between function and weight. This is not to say that all ultralight backpackers are the hiking equivalent of medieval penitents who crawl to pilgrimage sites on their hands and knees. Quite the contrary: Ultralight backpackers are single-mindedly aware of what gives them maximum comfort; it's just that for them, maximum comfort

This yucca isn't well-adapted to snow but has to survive it. The same might be said of light-weight backpackers.

equals the lightest possible pack. This is where you find the innovators—the people who dream up homemade alcohol stoves made of cat-food tins, or packs that use camping mattresses as part of the frame system. This is also where you sometimes find hikers taking risks. I have heard ultralight hikers talk about backpacking with no shelters, no raingear, and no stoves. (And indeed, I myself have backpacked with no shelter, no raingear, and no stove.) However, making such decisions requires a great deal of experience and very detailed knowledge about the place in which you plan to hike. It also requires a carefully considered back-up plan and conversations like this one:

"Okay, so we're agreed: The tent stays home. What do we do if it rains in the middle of night?"

"It won't. It's Arizona in May. It never rains."

"What do we do if it does?"

The answer can be many things: Get up in the middle of the night and start night hiking. Use the ground cloth and hiking sticks to rig a tarp. Camp near a road in case a quick bail-out is necessary.

But there's one thing the answer shouldn't be: "We never thought of that possibility."

The ultralight backpacker should have everything necessary for staying safe—just at a lighter than traditional weight. Sometimes (as, for example, when hiking in the Arizona desert in a typically dry month), you may hike perfectly happily, comfortably, and safely without certain items. But you need to do your homework. Most importantly, do not rely on other hikers' tales. Learn from them, yes—but filter them through your own experience and research.

Lightweight Hiking Issues and Challenges

Whenever lightweight backpacking is a topic at hiker gatherings, certain issues and concerns are sure to come up. Some are old myths that have assumed the mantle of authority by mere weight of repetition. Others are based on people's in-field experience. These issues all factor into a lightweight hiker's state of mind and gear-selection process. Let's look at them one by one.

Safety First?

The first question most people ask about lightweight hiking is "Is it safe?" Having lugged heavy packs for untold miles, they find it preposterous to think they can be safe with half the stuff or less.

If you stay at the more traditional end of the continuum, you basically substitute items on the basis of weight. Instead of a three-pound sleeping bag rated to thirty degrees, you may take a one-and-a-half pound bag with the same temperature rating. You're actually safer when you lighten your load this way. With a lighter pack containing exactly the same types of gear as you had before, you can move more quickly if necessary.

When you move into true lightweight hiking, however, you start making choices that could compromise both your comfort and your safety if you don't carefully research your decisions. For example, if you substitute a tarp for a tent, you should realize that a tarp does not offer as much protection in a rain-blowing-sideways sort of storm. So you need to know how to pitch a tarp so that the open sides are away from the wind, or how to choose a sheltered campsite. Without knowledge like this, lightweight camping can pose more risks than traditional camping. In a very real sense, the most important weight you carry is the gray matter inside your head.

Like the alpine mountaineers discussed above, lightweight and ultralight hikers must travel with a sharp eye on the weather and a flexible mindset. Going lightweight is not just about gear. It requires a willingness to change plans on a moment's notice. Perhaps you intended to camp high in the mountains with just a tarp and down sleeping bag. If a rainstorm is threatening, you may have to log a few more miles to a more protected spot. Nothing is wrong with this—unless you're someone who doesn't like changing plans, or you're not fit enough to put in a few extra miles at the end of the day. In either case, you could be miserable indeed, and might find yourself rethinking the whole idea of lightweight hiking.

You should also realize that ultralight hiking is *not* appropriate in all climates and environments. Many experienced hikers I've talked with use ultralight strategies only in moderate environments. (In fact, ultralight hiking gained its early popularity on the essentially dry Pacific Crest Trail, and is popular on the Appalachian Trail, where shelters are available about every 10 miles.) In certain climates and destinations, ultralight techniques simply won't work. Once, while hiking in New Zealand, I experienced twelve inches of rain in a forty-eight-hour period. I can tell you with absolute certainty that had I been out there with only a tarp and a down bag, I could easily have died of hypothermia. I can cite many other places where climates are reliably dangerous. Remember the comparison to the alpine mountaineer: The ultralight hiker cannot lay siege to his environment; he or she must understand that sometimes the mountain says "No."

Above all, be extremely careful when applying lightweight techniques above tree line. Mountains make their own weather systems, and the terrain above tree line is highly exposed, with very little shelter. Temperatures drop precipitously and winds increase, sometimes violently. To hike safely with a light pack, you need to be able to read your environment, evaluate your gear, and make appropriate decisions—which sometimes involve heading downhill, and sometimes involve taking more stuff.

To be safe, I recommend lightening up in steps and stages. You probably already have a closet filled with backpacking gear. Once you've read this book, you'll have a clear idea of which of your current gear is too heavy and which gear you can continue to use in a lightweight system. Start by replacing the heaviest gear and work your way down. Do some inexpensive experimentation: Practice setting up a tarp in the wind, and see if you're comfortable, warm, and dry underneath it. Borrow a closed-cell foam pad and see if you can sleep on it without aching bones.

Start in temperate climates. Note what happens and how you feel when the weather is bad. Over time, you'll learn what works for you, and you'll develop the skills and judgment to tackle more unsettled climates with ever lighter gear without risking your safety or ruining your trip.

Be Prepared—But for What?

A related criticism of lightweight hiking is that it violates the mantra we've all heard since childhood: Be prepared. To question this motto is akin to dissing motherhood and apple pie.

But what exactly should we be prepared for?

Some people carry more weight on day hikes than ultralight hikers pack for an entire trip. Are such heavily burdened day hikers better prepared? Not necessarily.

Being prepared is not a function of weight. A tiny photon flashlight weighing a fraction of the weight of the lightest headlamp, batteries included, provides enough light to read by, and even to hike by in an emergency. A miniature army knife about the size of a pen cap can do everything you need it to do, at a fraction the size of a traditional multifunction knife. A small compass identifies true north as accurately as a large one does. Just because a pack is lighter doesn't mean it doesn't contain what you need.

Storms roll in quickly above tree line. Lightweight hikers must keep a careful eye on the weather and be sure they have what they need to survive sudden storms.

"Be prepared" is a good basic motto, but it shouldn't mean being over-prepared. If you're hiking in July, you don't (usually) need to be prepared for a blizzard. If you're winter hiking in January, you don't have to carry mosquito repellent. This kind of "being prepared" is that old lay-siege-to-the-mountain philosophy at work. It suggests that a hiker should carry all sorts of extraneous gear just in case the improbable happens. If he steps on his waist-belt buckle, he has a spare. He has extra items in his first-aid kit just in case he stumbles across an injured hiker in the middle of the trail. He has more layers of clothing than he'll ever need. This hiker has read every backpacking book on the market, consolidated all the gear lists—and kept every single thing from every one of them. He is prepared for everything—except for having a good time.

Experienced hikers *are* prepared, but like alpine climbers, they define "being prepared" a little differently. They have appropriate gear for the conditions they can reasonably expect to occur as well as a few back-up items, especially when traveling in unsettled environments. Wherever they travel, they are prepared with knowledge of the destination—and with a plan for what to do if conditions deteriorate and create a dangerous situation. They are not afraid to turn back, to travel fast, or to change their plans. In addition to being prepared with the right gear, they are also prepared with knowledge.

The Comfort Conundrum

Many traditionalists, when introduced to the idea of lightweight hiking, protest: "Okay, so maybe you can survive. But how can you possibly be comfortable?"

Partly, the issue has to do with redefining comfort. We go into the backcountry in part to leave the material-filled industrial world behind. True, it is ironic that we use fabrics made of fossil fuels to do this, but the fact remains that most hikers are attracted to the simplicity of backcountry living.

Sometimes the idea of being uncomfortable is merely a lack of imagination. If you are carrying, for example, a thin, three-quarter-length closed-cell foam pad instead of a cushy, full-length air mattress, you may not be comfortable if you have to sleep on a field of gravel. That doesn't mean you can't be comfortable—it just means that you need to find campsites on softer ground. In many cases, comfort is as much about creativity as it is about gear.

Each of us will draw our own line in the sand. I am more than willing to put on a pair of damp, dirty socks in the morning, but I won't sleep in dirty clothes at night. Another hiker might insist that to be happy in the backcountry, he needs his backcountry pizza-making oven. Some hikers want the convenience of a reliable stove that boils water in three minutes flat; others don't mind futzing with a fire or waiting ten minutes for an alcohol stove to finally heat up. Of course, the more requirements we have, the heavier our packs will be.

But I won't sugarcoat this: There are many cases in which a lightweight hiker is, in fact, objectively less comfortable than his heavyweight partner. A thin pad *is* less comfortable than a thick one, a thirty-degree bag *is* less warm than a twenty-degree bag. How you deal with this, however, is a matter of attitude. Some hikers seem barely to notice the difference; others are highly sensitive. You may honestly be able to say that you are every bit as comfortable in your lightweight gear as you were with your heavy, traditional equipment. Your partner may feel exactly the opposite. It may be a matter of attitude, but in the end it doesn't really matter: You're both right about how you feel.

The Durability Debate

In my attic sits a pack that was state-of-the-art sometime in the late '80s. It's made of a high-count denier nylon that has stood up to cactus spines, cat's claws (the plant, not the panther), and the teeth of rummaging rodents. It has faded from the deep purplish blue it once was to the soft hues of a dying twilight, but every stitch is still in place. It has thousands of miles on it, and it might be good for thousands more. Although I long ago replaced it with a newer, more comfortable pack that fits me better, I keep it on hand as a back-up or to lend to the occasional weekend hiking partner who doesn't have a pack. It will probably live longer than I will. It weighs seven pounds.

Seven pounds—empty!

My old seven-pound pack represents the logical culmination of a trend that impacted backpacking gear through the seventies and eighties—a trend that still exerts a great deal of influence today. It's the trend of durability. The logic is obvious: If you're going to depend on your equipment in a place where replacements, spare parts, and repair shops are difficult, if not impossible, to find, you want to be sure your equipment is up to the task.

When they are not naming their products after feathers and breezes, manufacturers like to name their products after man-eating mountains like Denali, Everest, and K-2. They get ultra-runners and climbers and long-distance backpackers to endorse their products. They offer lifetime guarantees.

And it's not just hype. These products really do last. You may have stories to the contrary—there are always exceptions. But I can count on my fingers the times gear failure has caused me to alter my hiking plans. Given the mileage I've logged,

Going light in Nepal means carrying the appropriate gear for the high-altitude conditions.

I'd say that represents pretty good value in the durability department.

Manufacturers make bombproof gear because buyers—you and I—demand it. We want to know that our tent survived an avalanche on K-2, even if the only avalanches we are likely to see are the masses of memos dumped into our in-boxes every morning. As consumers, we also are demanding durability whenever we return products that don't last.

No doubt about it, durability is a desirable quality in a piece of gear you're going to be depending on out in the boonies. When you're in the back of beyond, you don't want your boot soles delaminating like peeling banana skins.

It's ironic that the marketplace insistence on durability is largely responsible for the overweight backpacks and tents we so often see. Manufacturers are caught in a bind: To compete with one another they must offer lifetime guarantees, which are an industry standard. That means that their gear has to be durable enough that consumers won't return it. But this kind of super-durability has a cost in weight because it requires heavier fabrics, reinforced seams, and additional patches at stress points.

Perhaps in the future, we'll see lightweight gear with more limited warrantees. It's hard to see how some of the most lightweight products now offered—for example, some of the one- and two-pound packs—can survive the kind of abuse typical of high-mileage hiking. But if these products are returned in high numbers because they rip and tear, manufacturers may no longer be able to offer them. Fortunately, new, high-tech materials are being introduced, such as Kevlar and Titanium, which are both lightweight and extremely durable. Many of these new products are, however, quite expensive.

It may be time to rethink the whole idea of durability. Are you better off buying a heavy pack that lasts five years and costs $500—or a much lighter pack that lasts one year and costs $100? Is it worth taking a chance with some new, lightweight, waterproof-breathable raingear that weighs less than a pound and costs only $70—but that probably won't last much longer than a season because it is made of such easily abraded fabric? At that price and weight, perhaps it's well worth purchasing, even without a lifetime guarantee. Perhaps durability is not always what we need from backpacking gear. Perhaps the lightweight mindset applies not only to choosing gear—but also to using it carefully and wisely.

Even the lightest equipment can last many seasons if it is cared for properly. It may be made of more fragile materials, but lightweight gear has fewer components to break, fewer zippers to jam, fewer seams to split. Obviously, your pack will last a lot longer if you set it on the ground (which is easier to do with a light pack) rather than drop it. A tent floor will last longer if you clean the site of protrusions before you pitch the tent. A lightweight backpack will last longer if it's not used for bigger loads than it was intended for.

Durability, in short, is important—but it is also something that we can increase ourselves, by choosing the right gear, and using it gently.

The Myth of Features

A friend of mine once called to tell me about a new backpack he had seen in a store. He went through a long description of its pockets and suspension system, its hip belt and its hydration pouch, and then he told me, "And it has a crampon guard!"

"That's nice," I said. "Do you have crampons?"

"No."

"Do you intend to get some or rent them?"

"No."

"Then why do you care that it has a crampon guard?"

Backpacking gear is not like an automobile! Features don't add value, they add weight. Extra zippers add weight, extra pockets add weight, gear compartments in tents add weight, extra straps add weight, crampon guards add weight. Some of these features are useful—sometimes. For example, I have a pair of Gore-Tex rain pants with full-length zippers and a thick draft tube that covers the zipper, preventing water leakage and cold-air seepage. These pants are great in high mountains in dangerous conditions, especially if I'm wearing crampons. But in the Sierra in August? No way are they worth the weight. The point is that you should be aware of which features you *really* need before you buy an overloaded piece of equipment.

Overcompensating

Most of us finally get around to learning from our mistakes, and this is a good thing—most of the time. The challenge for hikers is to learn from mistakes, to avoid repeating them, but not to overcompensate.

For example, if you were caught in the desert in a fierce and unexpected rainstorm, you might decide from then on to carry a full set of heavier raingear, a tent, and a pack cover every time you hike—even though you survived the rainstorm with your flimsier tarp, your not-quite-waterproof wind shell, and a pack you protected with a garbage bag. You might not consider that the chances of being caught in such a freak storm again are practically nil, and that even if you were to be in such a storm again, you'd survive it just fine the second time. Instead, you remember being wet and uncomfortable, and you want to prevent being wet and uncomfortable again. You've "learned your lesson."

Or maybe you remember the time you were caught in a three-day blizzard and your hiking partner—the one with the sixty-pound pack—had all those heavyweight creature comforts and rode out the storm with barely a shiver. So from then on, every time you hike, you take your complete storm gear, even if you are hiking on a dry weekend in a dry climate with a dry forecast. "You never know what might happen," you say, and you have the experience to prove it.

As time goes on, you keep "learning lessons"—and adding more gear. Of course, if you were dangerously unprepared and barely survived, then by all means, you should add gear. But most of the time, what is striking is how well prepared you

Lightweight hikers going above tree line should remember that secure shelter is often a long way down.

really were. An uncomfortable night is not a reason to overload your pack the next time. You also can learn from what you did right—and consider what you might have done to be even more comfortable. Could you have started a fire? Chosen a better tent site? Checked the weather forecast? Bailed out on a side route if only you had a map?

Ethics

I once hiked with a young woman who was very proud of her lightweight pack. She used a lightweight stove that worked fine in moderate but not freezing temperatures; she carried one pot that served as pot, bowl, and cup; she used a tarp instead of a tent; and she had a sleeping bag that was lightweight, but not very warm. Although she was supposedly hiking alone, I met her while she was in the company of several other hikers. I was curious about her light load, especially in the snowy, wet, cold conditions. Her secret was revealed to me one night when I saw her borrow a fellow hiker's stove and share tent space with another hiker.

Now, nothing is wrong with sharing gear with your hiking partner(s). It reduces everyone's pack weight. But this young woman wasn't sharing gear—she was using other people's gear.

Some hikers cut their gear to the bone, assuming that if they get in trouble, someone will step in to help. One friend of mine hikes the Appalachian Trail without a tent or a tarp, assuming that if a shelter is full, someone will make room or lend him their tent. Another hiker, wearing running shoes in the snowbound High Sierra, looked at my leather boots and said, "Oh, good, you have boots. You go first and kick the steps for the rest of us."

Neither the young woman nor the Sierra fast-packer premeditated using other people's gear; they just became opportunistic when the chance arose. The young woman carried enough to survive, and then solicited help from others to be more comfortable. The fast-packer would probably have made it over the pass just fine on his own, but kicking his own steps would have been more work—and more dangerous. In both cases, we're not talking about lightweight hiking, we're talking about mooching.

We've already discussed safety, but in the context of hiker ethics, it should be pointed out that every rescue puts people's lives in danger—not just the victim's, but also the rescuer's. At the very least, bailing you out of trouble is a huge inconvenience to other hikers. So when you head out with a lightweight pack, remember it is your responsibility to be sure you have what you need to be safe.

Nor should you rely on technology to bail you out. In recent years, cell phones have been added to the essentials kit of many hikers. If cell phones help you feel more secure, fine—but they shouldn't be regarded as a substitute for good judgment and appropriate gear. Also keep in mind that cell phones simply do not work in many hiking destinations. I live in Massachusetts, hardly the most remote state in the United States, and cell phones do not work reliably in the town where I live—let alone in the backcountry.

Lightweight Hiking: Is It for Everyone?

"Hike your own hike."

You'll hear this mantra on every long-distance trail. It simply means that no one right way exists for doing things. Lightweight hiking is not a whole-cloth philosophy. People's physical abilities vary, from the mileage they can do to the amount they sweat to how cold they get when they sleep. Their sensitivities vary. So do their preferences, their goals, and the environments in which they walk.

The only thing I'm sure of is that for every recommendation I make in this book, someone will disagree. If I suggest that you hike in running shoes, someone will write to me about getting a stress fracture that way. If I tell you to wear boots, a chorus will accuse me of old-fashioned, heavyweight thinking. If I recommend hiking sticks, I'll hear from someone who absolutely can't walk with them. However, no matter what your hiking style, I'm confident that lightweight hiking skills can help you have a better trip. I'm also confident that each hiker will have to find his or her own balance of lightweight skills, safety, comfort, and personal style. You may decide that a lightweight traditional pack suits your needs just fine, and that you don't want to make any additional gear changes to further reduce your pack weight. You like the privacy of a tent and the cooking options of your gas stove, and you feel more secure knowing you have full-coverage Gore-Tex for squalls above tree line. Even so, there are ways to reduce your pack weight to a more manageable load.

There are hundreds of ideas in this book. I don't use every single one on every hike, and nor should you. Take only those strategies that work for you. Cut a little, then cut a little more. Add back if you went past your comfort zone. Challenge yourself and your comfort zone, but not so much that you feel miserable. Hiking is about joy, and the purpose of lightweight hiking is not to reach some mythical perfect pack: It's to be more comfortable and happy on your hike. The perfect system is the one that helps you achieve this.

The main philosophy of this book is simple. Lightweight hiking strategies apply to everyone. They can help every hiker have a more enjoyable time in the backcountry. The less weight you have on your back, the more comfortable you will be on the trail.

However, as you consider the strategies offered here, keep the following in mind:
▲ You need the *right* stuff to keep you safe and comfortable in camp.
▲ You need a certain amount of *knowledge* (which will be provided in the remaining chapters) to choose and minimize the gear you use.
▲ Above all, you need to define and understand *your* hiking style and goals, and choose the techniques in this book that will help you reach them safely. Perhaps you want to hike 40 miles a day. Perhaps you want to hike 5 miles and sit in camp fishing and staring at the views. Perhaps you want to hike with your family. Perhaps you are fit, perhaps you aren't. Perhaps you hike in shaded forests; perhaps you hike in high mountains. All of these issues, and dozens more, will determine how you should apply and use the lightweight strategies that you'll find in this book as well as on hiker bulletin boards, in the hiking community, and in works by other writers.

Chapter 2

Strategies for a Lighter Load

oad lightening is a gradual process of trial and error. If you're a beginning backpacker, you need to familiarize yourself with the demands of outdoor living, and learn how different gear can help you cope with the various conditions you'll encounter. Eventually, you'll develop a personal hiking style, with your own preferences for gear, hiking environments, campsites, and the like. More experienced hikers have already developed their own styles, but now they need to experiment with new, lighter gear to see how it can meet their needs.

In this chapter, we get down to specific strategies for lightening the load.

Your Own Weight and Fitness

If you're serious about lightweight hiking, the place to start has nothing to do with your gear. Your first task is to step on a scale and weigh yourself. You know if the number you see is higher than you want it to be. For most of us, hiking light starts here.

Think about it this way: Your body consists of functional parts (muscles, bones,

Opposite: What's a good strategy for this rocky crest? (photo by Alan Bauer)

organs) and dead weight (extra fat). The functional parts keep you working and walking. Your organs and blood vessels keep you living; bones and muscle keep you moving.

Extra fat performs none of these tasks. Sure, a little bit of extra fat may help winter hikers stay warm, but for most of us, fat is simply something we have to carry. It puts the same stress on our heart and knees and ankles as would an extra sack of clothing or an extra bag of food. It makes us more prone to injury. It makes it harder to go uphill, harder to take a big step down, harder to haul ourselves up a rock scramble. Our hearts and legs don't care one whit if the extra forty pounds they are carrying consists of fat or backpacking gear—they still have to work harder than necessary.

Like alpine climbers, lightweight backpackers must be able to respond quickly to the environment—including sudden and unexpected changes in weather or trail conditions. Sometimes being safe means logging extra miles—to get out of exposed high country in a sudden storm, for example. This requires a high level of fitness, especially at the end of an already long day.

Most extreme ultralight hikers are in tip-top physical shape. They may not be professional athletes, but they are trim and fit. If you aspire to join their ranks, you need to be as trim as you want your pack to be.

This does not mean that you have to be an endurance athlete. Quite the contrary. A person in average shape has much to gain from using the gear-lightening strategies in this book. In fact, an overweight hiker quite possibly will appreciate the relief offered in these pages even more than his or her fitter hiking partner. But it is just plain dangerous for an unfit backpacker with limited experience to adopt ultralight techniques and then go out in a mountain storm. Cutting back on gear weight should be a gradual process.

A note to long-distance hikers: Don't assume that you'll get fit on the trail. Doing this guarantees you that your break-in days will be needlessly difficult. The early days are the most challenging for any hiker. By getting in shape before you even reach the trailhead, you'll make your trip more enjoyable from the very start.

Your Gear Weight—and Choices

Now that you've weighed yourself, let's talk about gear.

How much does your pack weigh when empty?

How much does your pack usually weigh when loaded up for a summer weekend?

How much does your sleeping bag weigh? What about your tent (stakes, poles, cords, and all)? And those camp shoes you carry around for comfort?

I'm willing to bet you don't know the answers. Most people groan under the weight of a too-heavy pack without having the slightest idea of what's causing it to be overweight. You may find that you've done a good job of saving weight in the major gear categories, but that your ditty bag is filled with ounces that have exploded into pounds of stuff that you barely ever use.

So the first thing to do is this: Go to the Gear–Weight Worksheets at the back of this book. Page 158 is for the hiker who typically hikes solo; page 160 is for those who typically hike as a couple. (Fill in both if you do both kinds of hiking.)

Using the worksheets, put together list of everything (and I mean everything, right down to your toothbrush) that you typically carry. I've listed the major gear categories to get you started, but don't feel compelled to fill in a line just because it's there. If you carry things I haven't listed, add those as well. (Note: Don't include food and water in the list. We'll talk about that later.)

Next, guess the weight of your gear.

A scale is your most important tool for lightweight packing! Before you can minimize your pack weight, you need to know what each item weighs.

You can bundle together items, such as your cooking gear, if that makes the guessing easier. But be sure everything is accounted for, right down to the pot scrubber. Add the numbers for your total pack weight.

Then, go to an office or kitchen supply store and buy either an inexpensive little postal scale or a kitchen scale. Get a scale that goes up to about five pounds and that measures ounces and half ounces. (As you'll learn later in this book, you should be thinking long and hard about taking any single piece of gear with you that weighs more than five pounds.) Some ultralight hikers use digital scales that measure fractions of ounces, but this is overkill for most hikers.

Once you have your scale, go back to the worksheet and fill in "Actual Weight", which asks you to weigh each individual piece of gear. If you previously gave the estimated weight of a collection of items, this time, break up those groups and weigh each item separately. Then add up the individual weights to arrive at a weight for the whole collection. To weigh a large piece of gear, such as a sleeping bag, on a postal scale, simply put it in a box and set the box on the scale. Subtract the weight of the box from the total weight.

Now add up the grand total of all your gear and compare it to your estimate. You may be surprised to see how inaccurate some of your guesses were. Notice which items were close to correct—and which ones were way off base. Note any items that seem disproportionately heavy. Does it make sense that your sleeping bag weighs three and a half pounds if you've heard that some people hike with entire backpacks that weigh less than ten pounds? Put check marks next to items that seem to be real weight hogs. These are the items you'll address first.

There's no right or wrong answer to what your total should be. What you typically carry is, of course, a function of where you typically hike: the climate, season, and terrain. It's also a function of the length of your hike, your experience, your comfort requirements, and your attitude, as well as other factors such as remoteness and whether or not you have a hiking partner. The point of this exercise is to orient you to where you currently are on the pack-weight continuum, and to get you thinking about the weight of every item you put in your pack.

One of the biggest contributions the lightweight backpacking movement has made is to create consumer awareness about the weight of backpacking gear. The vast majority of outdoor products available are overweight for their function. Seven-pound backpacks and six-pound tents are simply overkill for the conditions in which the vast majority of backpackers hike and camp—yet unwary consumers continue to purchase such products, not realizing that perfectly adequate alternatives are available for half those weights.

Think of the list you just made as the beginning of a weight budget, similar to a financial budget. You can't manage your money unless you know where you're spending it. Once you discover that you're spending $100 a month on gourmet lattes, it's easier to bring your budget under control. Same with pack weight.

Now that you've tallied the weight of all your gear, you need to find one more number. From the total, subtract the weight of the clothing and footwear you typically wear on the trail, as well as trekking poles (if you use them). What you have left is what we refer to as "base pack weight."

Base Pack Weight: The Magic Number

When a lightweight backpacker tells you he just hiked from Siberia to Australia with an eight-pound pack, he is usually referring to "base pack weight." This is the *fixed* weight of the gear on his back. It does not include food, water, or the clothes and footwear he is wearing.

Food and water are not inconsequential items; to the contrary, they add significant weight to a pack. However, the reason we use base pack weight as a measure is because variables like food and water make any meaningful discussion of pack weight worthless. One hiker may be finishing up a trip while another is heading out with fourteen days of food; another hiker may be starting a weekend trip in the desert, where she has to carry four liters of water. But remember, base pack weight is only part of what you carry: No one has yet managed to make food weight as light as a feather, and no matter what gear you buy, water will always weigh two pounds a quart. So even though this book, and other lightweight back-

Sharing gear with a partner reduces weight, but be sure you're committed to your partnership.

packing resources, refer to base pack weight, remember that when you are choosing a backpack, you will need to factor in both your base weight and the expected weight of your average food and water load.

Lightweight, Heavyweight, Ultralight: Which Are You?

Now that you know your base pack weight, what do you do with it?

First of all, knowing your base pack weight gives you an indication of where you stand on the lightweight–heavyweight continuum. The following figures are approximate, and assume that your hikes range from three-season treks in temperate forests to above–tree line treks in summer.

The Heavyweight: If your base pack weight weighs more than twenty-five pounds, give yourself a pat on the back for buying this book. If you apply just a few of the strategies you find here, I can promise you a more comfortable backcountry experience.

The Lightweight Traditionalist: If your base pack weight is in the eighteen-to twenty-five pound-range, you're probably an experienced hiker, but you're still using traditional gear. You've made some lightweight choices, and you've left a lot of extraneous stuff at home. But making some smart changes can significantly reduce your pack weight.

The Lightweight: Hikers with packs in the twelve to eighteen pound range are already skilled lightweight hikers. Chances are you've scoured the traditional manufacturers for their lightest offerings, and you're probably using a few pieces of less-traditional, lightweight equipment. You'll find more ideas here for other weight-saving strategies, as well as skills for maximizing the efficiency of the gear you already have.

The Ultralight Hiker: If your base pack weight is already below twelve pounds, you don't need this book.

Avoiding Weight Inflation

The second thing you use your list for is to keep your pack from developing the gear equivalent of middle-aged spread. You want to be sure that you never unknowingly substitute a heavier item for something that has worked for you in the past. This may sound like plain old common sense, but weight inflation is as insidious as inflation of the financial kind. Say you want to replace a tent that you've been happy with for the last five years. You go to the store and find the latest model, not even noticing that the manufacturer has added pockets and a little bit of floor space—and whoops! The weight is up by half a pound! Or perhaps you buy a new fleece jacket and don't even think about the weight of the extra pockets and zippers. Boom! You've added another quarter pound.

To keep weight inflation under control, keep your list handy. Also your scale, because whenever you are shopping for equipment, you should weigh whatever it is you plan to buy. (Note: You can also ask to use the store's scale. If they ever ship anything to anyone, they will have one.) You need to be sure that whenever you replace equipment, you replace it with something lighter.

Be rigorous about this. You can't necessarily count on manufacturers' stated weights. They are often inaccurate, and when they are, they are usually understated. Sometimes this is because of manufacturing irregularities. Sometimes it is because a manufacturer will provide a number of components in the package, but will count only some of them as the gear's "field weight." However, the definition of "field weight" is not consistent among manufacturers and may not have anything to do with what you yourself actually carry into the field. (For example, some tent "field weights" include only the tent and poles, but not the stakes or cords.) To get an accurate weight, you need to weigh the gear yourself.

Monitoring Your Base Pack Weight

The third use for your list is as a monitoring device. One rule of lightweight backpacking is, "If you don't use it, you have to lose it." If you're serious about lightweight hiking, try keeping a log or a notebook, much as scuba divers do. Divers note condi-

Use gear that does double duty: In this case, a trekking pole during the day becomes a tent support at night.

tions, what gear they were using, and how they felt on the dive: On subsequent dives, they use this information to help them select the right gear and plan a better dive.

In your log, note how many days you hiked, weather and terrain, how much food you took (and how much you brought back), how much stove fuel you used (and brought back), what gear you used and didn't use and how it performed, and whether you were lacking any gear. After keeping a log like this for enough hikes, you'll discover what gear you need to keep carrying and what gear you can leave home. For example, you might discover that you've never worn your rain pants, even in the biggest downpour you experienced. So you can probably leave those rain pants at home. On the other hand, if you consistently note that you were cold at night, you'll probably want to either get a warmer bag or carry an extra layer of clothing to sleep in.

You should also make a list of emergency must-have gear. This is your "essentials and emergencies" kit, which should include such things as the "ten essentials" and foul weather gear appropriate for the conditions (see Chapter 7, Sweating the Small Stuff). Items in this carefully considered emergency kit are exempt from the "if you don't use it, you have to lose it" rule. They are not, however, exempt from reevaluation and replacement as newer lighter options become available, or as your confidence and skills increase.

Lightweight Strategies

Once you have determined what you are already carrying and how much it weighs, you are ready to move on to the next phase: lightening your load.

Do You Need It? Really? Why? What will happen if you don't have it? What is the worst that *could* happen? Is that likely to happen? What could you do if it does? Would it ruin the trip for you? Are there any alternatives? What other gear are you carrying that might be useful?

These questions are intended to get you thinking about your needs and what it takes for you to have an enjoyable experience. If sleeping in a tarp in wet clothes would ruin the trip for you, then by all means, take along extra clothes or a tent. If one of the highlights of hiking for you is nestling into your sleeping bag with a good book in the evening, then take along the book (paperback, please). Hiking is recreation. It's about fun, and enjoyment, not deprivation. The trick is identifying which things truly give you joy, and which ones you are unthinkingly taking out of habit.

Don't Over-Equip: You don't need a twenty-degree bag if the lowest temperature you'll ever sleep in is a balmy forty-five degrees. You don't need head-to-toe coverage in a Gore-Tex rain suit to hike in the Sonoran Desert in May. Yes, you need to carry the common-sense basics. But don't pack that winter three-person tent unless you are hiking in winter with two hiking partners.

Take Advantage of New Technology: New technology and new designs are lightening gear all the time. Some of these high-tech items are expensive, but if they are both durable and lightweight, they may be worth the price. Check the Internet for new designs (see Resources at the end of this book for some recommended sites). Some of the most cutting-edge equipment is being made by small mom-and-pop companies, which are often headed by long-distance hikers with inventive minds.

Make Your Own: While making your own lightweight gear is beyond the scope of this book, it may be something to consider once you have exhausted the realm of commercially available gear (although the vast majority of hikers find that there is more than enough gear available from manufacturers to meet their needs). If you are interested in experimenting with homemade gear, you'll find patterns on the Internet (see Resources at the end of this book for some recommended sites). Most popular items include homemade alcohol stoves, stuff sacks, sleeping coverlets, and clothing.

Start with low-tech, low-design products, such as stuff sacks, which are not subject to a lot of wear and tear, and for which malfunctions have limited consequences. A sleeping sack and a tarp are both relatively easy. Tents are much more difficult. Save backpacks for last—if ever. Making something as complicated as a backpack is too difficult for most people, and a malfunctioning backpack could cause not only inconvenience, but even injury.

Opposite: Backcountry refuges offer shelter and may eliminate the need to carry a tent.

Use Items That Can Serve Multiple Purposes: Anything that can do more than one job earns its way in your pack. Trekking poles can act as tarp supports or as poles for tepee tents. Extra socks can double as gloves. A wicking shirt can be wrapped around your neck as a scarf. Bandannas can be used for everything from wiping your nose to holding a hot pot. Candles can be used to light a shelter or to help start a fire. Duct tape fixes (almost) everything.

Cut the Extra Features: If your gear has extra features that you aren't using, cut them off. You won't save much weight this way, but you will have a satisfying pile of refuse to point to. Candidates for cutting include extra-long straps and cords (seal with a match so they won't unravel), extra daisy chains and loops on your pack, anything that dangles, fabric tags, and modular pouches you don't need for that particular trip. (See Chapter 7, Sweating the Small Stuff, for more ideas and a few cautionary notes.)

Repackage and Measure: Food packaging is unnecessary, adds weight, and takes up space in your pack. Also, the packaging rarely contains the exact amount that you will need on a particular trip. Repackage food in zipper-lock bags whenever possible, measuring everything and taking only what you will use. Measure and repackage even small amounts of items such as dried cheese, spices, powdered milk, and sugar.

Measure and repackage nonfood consumables, too. Use little plastic containers for toothpaste or ointments. Also consider how much water and fuel you are carrying, and take only what you need.

Use Resupplies and Floaters on Longer Hikes: Break up a ten-day hike into two five-day stretches, or an eight-day hike into two four-day stretches. You can mail yourself a box of supplies in care of general delivery at a town near the trail. If you are long-distance hiking, look at the legs of your journey—the sections between each resupply point—as individual mini-hikes. Yes, you may need your ice ax for that alpine stretch that starts next week, but if you don't need it this week, ship it ahead in a "floater" box. Using floater boxes can save long-distance hikers several pounds of pack weight.

Travel with a Partner: Couples and committed hiking partners can make out like bandits in the weight-reduction game by sharing shelters, stoves, cooking gear, and ground cloths. You can also share an emergency kit, some hygiene supplies, and a repair kit. Some couples additionally share large sleeping bags or use sleeping bag doublers (see Chapter 4, Oh, for a Good Night's Sleep: Sleeping Bags).

If you do share gear with a partner, divide everything is such a way that if you get separated, the gear can still be used. For example, if one of you carries the stove and matches and the other carries the pots and fuel, neither of you will have a hot dinner if you get separated. Likewise, if one person carries the tent, including stakes and poles, the other person should carry the ground cloth, which could be used as an emergency shelter.

Choose the lightest gear that does the job. This tarp tent provides shelter from both weather and insects.

Chapter 3

Give Me Shelter: Tents

T here is nothing new, of course, about humans using portable lightweight shelters. Our ancestors made use of poles from trees and skin from animals. Today, we use high-tech materials such as silicone-impregnated nylons, aluminum, and titanium. But whether it's yurts, tepees, or army tents, the idea hasn't changed since the dawn of humanity: We need something to keep the weather out and the heat in.

It's quite a challenge.

We humans are a sensitive species. Let the temperature dip much below sixty-eight degrees, and we start rummaging around for sweaters to fend off the chill. When the mercury inches ten degrees higher, most of us start perusing ads for air-conditioner.

This sensitivity is not merely a matter of comfort. Our internal regulatory systems are so acutely calibrated that a shift of only a few degrees in our average core temperature of 98.6 can lead to heat stroke or hypothermia, both potentially deadly conditions.

Rain and wind exacerbate the problem. Cold water wicks warmth away from our skins eight times faster than cold air alone. Add a little wind, and the warmth vanishes like ice cream in summertime. The twin realities of outdoor living are

Opposite: Home-sweet-home on the trail. (photo by Alan Bauer)

these: Human bodies are vulnerable, and Mother Nature is stronger than we are.

But at the same time, using their ingenuity, humans can comfortably sleep outside when the temperature is well below zero. It doesn't even take high-tech equipment. As a species, we've been able to survive arctic winters and entire ice ages. In this chapter, we look at portable shelters—something our ice age cousins knew well. But the designs and lightweight equipment available to us today would boggle their minds.

Traditional Thinking, Traditional Tents

Let's start with a brief look at the traditional tent, the kind you (or your parents) might remember from childhood scouting days. The so-called pup tent was a simple A-frame. Details varied, but the standard A-frame tent had a floor connected to the body or sides, and some sort of rain fly. The steep slope of the A-frame design encouraged water to run quickly off the tent roof. A ridge pole held the tent up; stakes and cords secured it to the ground.

The whole design was a picture of compromise. The tent provided shelter, but at the expense of both comfort and weight. The shape offered minimal headroom, the fabric walls made the tent airless and stuffy, and the tent was relatively heavy for the floor space.

Evolution of new materials and the influence of mountaineering gave tent designers free rein to improve the design of the traditional pup tent. Designers modified the A-frame into a wind-shedding wedge, or abandoned it altogether by adapting mountaineering-inspired designs such as the dome or the tunnel. The

Traditional lightweight tents: The North Face Slickrock weighs about 5.5 pounds and sleeps two people comfortably, but the minimal rain fly is challenged by severe storms.

inner layer of a traditional tent became thinner and thinner, in some cases little more than mosquito netting.

At the same time, though, backpackers started demanding more and more features, such as better headroom, pouches for storing and organizing equipment, vestibules for cooking or for storing wet gear and boots, zip-away windows, "stargazing" mosquito netting, and loops for hanging candle lanterns. Most of these features added weight, so as tents became more luxurious, they also became heavier.

Which brings us to the new millennium. *Backpacker* magazine's annual Gear Guides now list hundreds of tents, ranging from simple tarps to multiperson palaces. Buying a tent isn't quite as confusing as buying a house—but it's more confusing than in the days of the pup tent.

Assessing Your Needs

With tents, the tradeoffs are obvious: A tent that is roomy and comfortable in camp is heavy to carry on the trail.

For lightweight hikers, this is the central issue—and only you can decide where you want your comfort. Will you be spending long hours on the trail banging out big miles? Or lazy hours lounging around a lakeside campsite? If the first, comfort on the trail is probably your priority, and you should choose a lightweight shelter. If the second, you might spring for roomier quarters at the price of a heavier pack.

When thinking about tents, many hikers consider everything that could possibly happen and then prepare for the worst. Indeed, this is the traditionalist's way of thinking. But lightweight hikers think a little differently, questioning the likelihood of a summer storm confining them to a tent for three days—or even one day. The fact is, for average hikers in average conditions, dramatically dangerous weather conditions are as rare as a hippopotamus in the Sahara. Think about it: Have you ever been tentbound for days?

Another example: How often have the bugs been so bad that they confined you to your tent all day? In most cases, you have choices when it comes to campsites, and you can choose sites that aren't overrun with mosquitoes or other pests. Sometimes you'll want and appreciate the space of an oversized tent, but those times are, for most backpackers, either few and far between—or completely avoidable.

The bottom line is this: You *must* carry some sort of shelter to ensure your survival should the worst happen—but whether it also ensures your *comfort* is optional. Do you choose comfort for the vast majority of your hiking days by carrying a lightweight tent or tarp shelter, or do you choose optimum camp comfort for that once-in-a-blue-moon disaster—at the price of lugging a heavier pack day after day? Many lightweight hikers feel that a night of minor discomfort once in a while is a fair price to pay for hundreds of miles of comfortable lightweight hiking. Or do you compromise? After all, it's not an all-or-nothing choice.

Two of the most popular lightweight tents are the North Face Tadpole (front) and Sierra Design's Clip Flashlight. Both are weather-worthy, but sacrifice space for weight.

Hundreds of tents exist between the extremes of a jerry-rigged emergency space blanket and a full-featured tent.

Only you can be the judge of what is acceptable risk and acceptable discomfort.

Short-Distance Hikers

As with many categories of equipment, hikers traveling short distances have an advantage when it comes to choosing tents, particularly if they are hiking close to home. If you hike locally, you can pick your weekends according to the weather forecast. You still need a shelter in case the weather forecast is wrong, but if the forecast is for several days of bright sunshine, you're unlikely to need a tent designed for monsoon season in the tropics. Similarly, if you know your region, you know when bug season is and can avoid it (or take the appropriate gear). It's easier to fine-tune and lighten your gear when you know the terrain and climate—and have the option of avoiding inclement conditions all together.

Long-Distance Hikers

Long-distance hikers have different problems because for the most part, they can't simply change their plans and go home if a rain storm hits—they have to keep walking no matter what. Also, conditions can vary dramatically from week to week as the terrain changes. Finding lightweight gear that can handle the vast range of conditions one encounters on long trails can be difficult.

Changing gear en route is one solution. For example, on the Pacific Crest Trail, most hikers prefer to use tarps in Southern California, where bugs are not a problem at night. However, during snowmelt in the Sierra, mosquitoes can be fierce, and all but the most devoted (and thick-skinned) lightweight hikers will find the weight of a shelter with mosquito-netting worthwhile. Later, in Northern California and Oregon, when the height of bug season has passed and the weather is reliably dry, many hikers switch back to tarps. If they hike on into the North Cascades during rainy season, they may switch back to tents. Of course, such strategies require a great deal of planning.

A Tent for All Seasons?

Shelters can vary from a full-fledged four-season mountaineering tent complete with cook-holes, storm flaps, and poles that are strong enough to bear heavy snow loads, to an emergency tube-tent weighing little more than few ounces. The tube-tent would be hopelessly inadequate on the slopes of Washington's Mount Olympus during the rainy season. But a four-season monolith would be equally out of place on the Appalachian Trail in June. Not only would it be unnecessarily heavy, but it wouldn't provide the ventilation and airflow a hiker needs in hot conditions.

Thus, the commonly used term "four-season tent" is a misnomer. No tent is going to work at peak efficiency in all four seasons. Three-season tents generally handle moderate spring, summer, and fall conditions, although some can handle a light dusting of snow as well. Winter tents take on the fourth season. Summer tents

The North Face Tadpole provides good protection against both rain and mosquitoes but, at about 5 pounds, is a better choice for two hikers sharing a shelter than a solo backpacker.

are flimsier (and lighter), with lots of mosquito netting and abbreviated rain flys. They don't provide storm-proof shelter, but if you are hiking in temperate conditions, they may be just the ticket. So take some time to determine what seasons you prefer and what weather conditions you encounter most often. Then select the tent that will give you the most protection and comfort in those conditions—for the least amount of weight.

Shelter from What?

Before shopping for a tent, stop a moment to think about what you need it to do. What, precisely, do you need to be sheltered from?

Rain

In most hiking destinations—unless you live in, say, Arizona—rain is the number one condition you need to consider when choosing a tent. Especially in the mountains, it's foolhardy to backpack without carrying something, if only an emergency shelter, to cover yourself if it rains at night. As we all know, weather forecasts are not always reliable. They are even less reliable in the places in which hikers like to travel. Even low mountains create their own weather systems, which means that a local valley weather forecast may not apply to your hiking destination in the hills.

All shelters, with the exception of simple bug nets, can repel rain, but some are better suited for light drizzles than for long downpours. Your first questions should be: Do I hike in places where rain is common? How serious is the rain—light drizzles or horizontal sheets? Can I (and will I) cancel my hiking trip or hike out at the first sign of rain, or will I march on rain or shine? The answers to these questions will determine whether you choose a tent with down-to-the-ground rain-fly coverage, or a lighter, more airy tent with less coverage but more exposure.

Snow

For three-season backpackers, snow is less of a concern when choosing a tent. Theoretically, it can snow any day of the year above tree line. But in most of the forty-eight contiguous states, this is a rare (though not impossible) occurrence.

Most three-season hiking tents can handle a little bit of snow. The steeper the roof, the better the tent's ability to shed snow. Wedge-shaped tents, popular among three-season hikers, are too flat to shed snow effectively. If you get stuck in snow while using one, you'll have to bang the snow off the roof when it accumulates. Also be aware that tents with partial rain-fly coverage and lots of mosquito netting may let in blowing snow. Even so, you will be able to sit out the rare summer snow squall in a three-season shelter, especially if you pay attention to wind direction and the availability of natural snow breaks such as tress and large rocks. Even a properly pitched tarp can handle snow, although you'll need to pitch it low and close to the ground to keep out as much blowing snow as possible.

| | | |

Camping Warmth and Comfort

Knowledge of some basic mountain weather patterns can help you choose a more comfortable campsite, whether you are looking for coolness, warmth, breeze, or wind protection.

Cold air (also called katabatic air) tends to collect in valley bottoms due to the simple law of physics that warm air rises. This is especially true near streams that flow along valley floors. In hot weather, sites along a valley floor can be noticeably cooler—ten or twenty degrees cooler—than sites just forty or fifty feet higher, on a rim or a ridge. However, make sure you are not camped in the bottom of a dry streambed—a flash flood is sometimes a possibility, albeit a remote one in most regions.

Conversely, in cooler weather, you will want to avoid the valley bottoms and head uphill a bit. But not too far! The crest of a ridge or a high pass acts as a wind tunnel. A small knoll is a good choice if you want a breeze to blow insects away, but an exposed pass may provide more wind than you want or need.

Wind and Cold

Tents provide an element of extra warmth by blocking wind and providing a sheltered airspace around a sleeping person. The more people you have in a tent, the warmer the tent. However, condensation can be a problem if too much hot air collects. Properly pitched tarps don't trap warmth, and thus don't have a condensation problem; they do offer wind protection.

Sun and Heat

A closed tent can be unbearably hot in warm weather. If you usually hike in midsummer, you'll want a tent with as much open netting as possible. (Good news: This reduces a tent's weight.)

Or take a tarp. Some hikers use tarps to shelter themselves from the midday heat of desert hiking, stringing the tarp between a couple of scrubby creosote bushes to create a little shade to rest in. However, don't expect much relief. By midday, the ground has usually absorbed so much heat that the difference isn't quite what you might have hoped for. Far better (and cooler) is to take a midday break under a live oak or a cottonwood. Shade clothes are another strategy for sun protection.

Insects

As important as rain protection is protection from insects. Mosquitoes are the main problem, since biting flies usually retire at dusk. Campsite selection is one way to minimize mosquito problems. Stay away from standing water and meadows, and look for breezy sites. But in the height of mosquito season (usually just following the snowmelt), you may be vastly more comfortable in a fully protected tent or a tarp with good insect rigging. (Clothing selection can also help.)

Scorpions, Snakes, and Other Critters

It seems a natural human desire to draw a curtain of protection around us in the dark scary night—even if that protection is merely a thin sheet of nylon. However, most denizens of the night are not inclined to come investigating.

Scorpions may occasionally make themselves at home in your boots or might crawl into an unoccupied sleeping bag while you're off somewhere watching the sunset, so it's a good idea to check your sleeping bag before climbing in, and to shake out your boots in the morning before you put your feet inside. Skunks and raccoons may come a-calling in popular campsites, particularly if you've left food out. Properly storing your food will usually eliminate this problem. Desert hikers worry about nocturnal rattlesnake visits, but I've never heard of a rattlesnake snuggling up against a hiker. (That's not to say it can't happen, but after hiking more than 2000 desert miles, I've put it far down on my list of concerns.)

For the most part, wild animals aren't interested in interspecies encounters with us humans—especially in remote campsites. In frequently used areas, animals are more habituated to humans, and you may prefer a tent. The lightweight alternative is to choose less-popular campsites where animals are less likely to come looking for handouts.

The Eureka Gossamer provides one person with good shelter against both bugs and storms at a weight of about 3 pounds.

Prying Eyes

Women traveling alone may especially appreciate a shelter that offers privacy, so their solo state is not on display to every passerby. But you don't necessarily need a tent for privacy. Good campsite selection is more than half the battle. Look for natural walls such as hedges, small ridges, or copses of trees, and camp where you are out of sight from the trails.

Tent Types

Tents come in one-person, two-person, three-person (or even more) styles. If you're traveling in a group, you can save weight by taking a three-person tent instead of a one-person tent plus a two-person tent. Before you go for the three-person tent, however, ask yourself: Do you really want to live in such intimate quarters with those guys?

Lightweight Traditional Tents

The majority of backpackers choose tents as their primary means of shelter for good reasons. A traditional tent offers enormous advantages in terms of flexibility and protection, including bug protection, rain protection, warmth, privacy, wind resistance, and ease of set-up. If you expect to deal with a wide variety of climate and bug conditions, a tent is certainly the easiest and most protective shelter you can choose.

Despite the hundreds of types of tents on the market, one single factor will slash your choices considerably. A lightweight tent for two people should weigh no more than five and a half pounds—ideally, it should weigh around four pounds (or less). Only a small percentage of tents meet this standard, and they are the *only* ones you should consider for three-season hiking. (The only exceptions to this would be extremely tall people who don't fit in an average-sized tent, or people planning trips in highly unusual conditions. And to be honest, I can't think of any three-season conditions that would require a heavier tent.)

Understand that a two-person tent weighing five and a half pounds or less lacks some of the extras heavier tents advertise so proudly. Most lightweight tents have two poles instead of three, so they aren't freestanding and will require staking. But the rain flys on most freestanding tents have to be staked out anyway. And places where stakes are difficult to drive into the ground usually have plenty of rocks and trees that can be used for tying off the tent.

Lightweight tents may not have adequate headroom for sitting up, or the floor space may be so tight that your nose ends up in your partner's armpit. There may be no space for a vestibule—and no space for most of your gear. An inner layer made mostly of mosquito netting may be great for ventilation (and weight savings), but it can allow cold and wind-whipped rain to penetrate. A tent with a rain fly that doesn't come all the way down to the ground will be airier and lighter—but it also may be wetter.

That said, a well-designed lightweight tent chosen for the conditions you expect to encounter usually provides adequate and comfortable shelter. Some features to look for: a bathtub floor, which brings the waterproofing several inches up from the ground; a vestibule for storing wet gear; lots of netting for bug protection and ventilation; and enough headroom to sit up.

A warning about the use of the word "lightweight": Manufacturers often play fast and loose with the term, applying it to tents that weigh as much as six pounds or more. But sayin' so don't make it so. Don't rely on an advertisement or product tag. Do some comparison shopping, use *Backpacker* magazine's annual Gear Guide, and take your postal scale along when you shop to see what the packed weight of the tent actually is. I have on more than one occasion been astonished at the difference between the manufacturer's stated weight and the weight registered on a postal scale.

Two-Hoop Tents

One of the most popular lightweight tents on the market is the two-hoop design, which can weigh in at less than four pounds for two people. These tents are the traditionalist's approach to lightweight camping, and they can be reasonably light on the wallet, too. Two-hoop tents are not freestanding, but they require only a couple of stakes to keep them earthbound. There is limited floor space, but decent headroom, and a small amount of vestibule space.

Three-Pole Wedge-Shape Tents

The three-pole wedge-shape tent design was introduced with Northface's popular Tadpole back in the '80s, a four-and-one-half-pound tent that numerous other companies proceeded to copy. It remains a favorite among long-distance hiking couples because it is freestanding, relatively lightweight, has a vestibule, and offers the most effective weather protection: If you're heading for the Scottish Highlands or the French Pyrenees or the North Cascades or New Zealand's South Island (all places where they know how to make storms), this is definitely a tent to consider. And in less severe weather, you can leave the interior body of the tent at home and just pitch it with the rain fly and the poles. However, the stingy interior space makes this tent uncomfortable for platonic partners, especially large guys.

Dome Tents

Also worth a look are lightweight modified domes, at around five and a half pounds. Features vary. A dome with a door on either side of the tent allows occupants to exit the tent without tripping over each other. The dome shape has an inherent disadvantage, however. Without a cleverly designed rain fly, the doors often let in rain when you open the doors to exit the tent. Most domes lack vestibule space, but some have a mini-vestibule under the rain fly, where gear can be tucked away. Northface's Slickrock saves weight by using a waterproof single-layer fabric for part of the tent, and a small rain fly for the rest. It's not weather-worthy in heavy storms—

Moonbow's unique Gourmet opens up to offer a dining awning. The tent is part of a system that incorporates a backpack, ground cloth, tent, and sleeping bag—all for under 10 pounds.

especially if there is wind and back-splashing rain—but it withstands an average rainy night just fine and provides lots of ventilation. This tent also has enough headroom and interior space for two people to sit up at the same time, which makes it easier to change clothes, pack, and dine inside.

Single-Wall Tents

Single-wall tents apply a common-sense approach to the job of lightening the weight of a tent: They use less fabric. While traditional tents have an inner layer of breathable fabric (sometimes largely mosquito netting) and an outer layer of water-proof fabric, the single-wall tent has merely one layer of fabric, which is supposedly both waterproof and breathable. In a traditional tent, air-flow between the two layers takes care of most ventilation and condensation problems. In a single-wall tent, warm air is supposed to escape through the breathable fabric. This works better in theory than in practice, and it also works better in cold dry climates than in warm wet ones. Hikers consistently complain of condensation problems with single-wall tents in temperate conditions. In the kind of warm humid weather that brings out the bugs, you may find that taking refuge in your single-wall tent is almost as unbearable as dealing with the mosquitoes.

Single-wall tents are considerably lighter than traditional tents, with two-person styles weighing in at as little as three pounds. Solo models are available for as little as two pounds. But as weight goes down, price goes up. Expect to pay at least $300 and possibly more than $800.

One-Person Tents and Bivvy Tents

One-person tents save weight, but they can be claustrophobic. Most have lower headroom than two-person tents, which makes it difficult, if not impossible, to sit up inside. If you're stuck indoors in bad weather, you might be in for some long, cramped afternoons and inconvenient in-tent dining. When checking out tents—either one-person or two-person styles—crawl inside (with your hiking partner, if you have one) and feel out the space. People taller than average may find their heads and legs bumping up against the edges.

Bivvy tents are even smaller and tighter than one-person tents. While a true one-person tent may have a vestibule and at least a little headroom; a bivvy tent covers only your sleeping bag, and may have a small hoop that holds up the rain sheet and gives you a precious few inches of headroom. Forget about eating inside (let alone cooking).

As with single-wall tents, bivvies offer bug protection, but the cost can be sweltering airless discomfort, and, not infrequently, tremendous condensation. Bivvy sacks have their origins on high mountain slopes, and, like single-wall tents, that's where they are most successfully used. In warmer humid weather (like your basic mosquito-infested forest in summertime), they are simply too wet, hot, and humid. They are most appropriate for colder weather, as emergency backups, or perhaps for a solo hiker in alpine conditions, where a tarp would be difficult to use.

Non-Tents and New Tents

Protective, they might be, but tents have four major disadvantages, which have led to the evolution of tent-alternatives.

The first disadvantage is, of course, weight. There is simply no way that a tent is going to weigh as little as a tarp.

The second disadvantage is ventilation. A tightly closed tent on a warm, humid, thunder-stormy night can be about as comfortable (and smelly) as a steamroom.

The third disadvantage is that a tent effectively seals you off from the outdoors you are trying to experience and enjoy. Some tents have bug-netting "windows" and "skylights" that offer protection from insects while maintaining a room with an only somewhat shrouded view, but a tarp puts you in closer contact with the natural world.

The fourth disadvantage is price. Compared to tarps, some tents put as much stress on your budget as they do on your back.

These disadvantages have led both hikers and manufacturers to experiment with alternate designs such as modified tents, tarp-tents, and tarps, which meet the needs of many hikers at minimal weight and cost.

Tarps

The humble tarp is a model of elegant simplicity. Lightweight, inexpensive, and functional, a well-pitched tarp does exactly what it needs to do—no more, no less. It provides basic wind and rain protection in most temperate three-season conditions, and if skillfully pitched, it can handle more serious conditions as well.

But tarps aren't for everyone.

First, it takes practice to pitch a tarp. If you haven't done it before, you'll need to take a trial run—or two or three or four—in your yard.

Second, a tarp does not provide the kind of near-total protection that a tent does. Pitch it with its open side facing the wind, and you might find yourself covered with wind-blown rain or snow. And wind direction can change during the night!

Third, while tents provide at least an illusion of protection from the great black night, with a tarp, you are disconcertingly close to any wandering wildlife. Usually, the wildlife stays far away, but the perceived proximity can take some getting used to.

And fourth, there are those annoying mosquitoes. A tarp without some sort of mosquito netting is not going to give you any protection against six-legged drill-nosed blood-suckers.

A tautly pitched tarp provides shade as well as rain protection. This 72-square-foot tarp was capacious for two people and weighs about 1.5 pounds, including stakes and cord.

That said, some hikers have successfully completed multi-thousand–mile trails relying solely on a tarp. Most of them have tales to tell about a few uncomfortable nights, but they opted for on-trail comfort versus total comfort every night in camp. I would never, for instance, recommend a tarp for any mountain area during snowmelt. But some hikers are more willing to put up with mosquitoes than I am, and they survive bug season just fine with the help of full-coverage clothing, a head net, some repellent, and a positive attitude. Your willingness to make these tradeoffs is something you'll have to decide for yourself.

A tarp is basically a big flat sheet of waterproof nylon—more often, two sheets sewn together. (Note: If there are seams, they must be sealed just as you would with any unsealed seams in a tent.) The tarp is pitched by suspending it, using trees, trekking poles, or sticks found in the woods. Loops of cords secured with stakes hold the edges in place on the ground. There is no "floor," so you need to bring a ground cloth. Tarps come in different sizes. An eight-by-eight-foot (or seven-by-nine) tarp is big enough for two adults; an eight-by-nine-foot tarp is almost luxuriously large, with lots of room to spread out gear. A square foot of silicone-impregnated nylon weighs about half an ounce, so the extra space is inexpensive from a weight standpoint. The larger the tarp, the more weather protection it affords. A larger tarp can be pitched all the way to the ground, and you can escape any stray wind-borne raindrops by sleeping near the center with plenty of fabric to protect you.

The lightest tarps are made of silicone-impregnated nylon. Tarps are available from a variety of outlets including Campmor, Oware, Integral Designs, and GoLite.

Tarp-Tents

Tarp-tents are a step up in complexity and function from basic flat-sheet tarps, adding protection at the cost of only a few ounces. Essentially, the flat shape of a tarp gives you a limited number of ways to pitch it. A tarp-tent has a few extra pieces of material sewn into place that provide a little extra protection. There may be a beak over the front, or a flap that folds over at the back, or the tarp may be sewn so that when pitched, it falls into place looking more like a traditional tent. In short, tarp-tents are fancies of functional geometry that make each plane and angle work harder for you in terms of weather protection. Some tarp-tents come with inner liners of mosquito netting; some require the use of trekking poles for set-up.

Floorless Tents and Tepee Tents

Lighter than traditional tents and heavier than tarps, floorless tents provide good protection from wind and hard, driving rain. Bug protection is minimal, even with a mosquito net, because bugs will get in through and around the dirt and grass. Some floorless tents have optional floors that can be zipped into place, although

This tarp-tent uses a trekking pole for support.

these usually bring the weight of the whole contraption up to the weight of a traditional tent.

The advantage of a system like this is its flexibility. GoLite's Hex 3, for example, is basically a fabric tepee weighing just over two pounds that can be pitched using trekking poles. The Hex 3 sleeps up to three people. Optional extras include an inner tent of mosquito netting and an attachable tent floor (two pounds, six ounces). You can use the tent fly alone in light rain, add the bug net when it's mosquito season, and add the floor when conditions turn truly awful.

Hammock-Tent Systems

Another unusual but ingenious category of shelters is the backpacking hammock, which usually consists of a mesh hammock for sleeping on and an overhead, integrated tarp for rain protection.

Advocates of hammocks point to their weight, which can be as low as fifteen ounces including hammock, bug net, and rain fly. But you have to like sleeping in them, and not everybody does. Hennessey Hammocks makes backpacking hammocks that are designed to help you sleep in a fairly flat position.

Hammocks have some interesting advantages. First, they help redefine your notion of an appropriate tent site. The ground can be sloping at thirty degrees and

Hammock tents can be pitched anywhere there are trees and provide decent one-person shelter from insects and weather.

it doesn't matter as long as you can find two trees. Nor does it matter if the ground is rocky or filled with tree stumps. If you have trees, you have a campsite.

Two issues with hammocks: Pitching requires trees. It also requires familiarity with the ropes and knots. Setting up a secure hammock takes a little time, at least at first. But the main issue some hikers have with hammocks is staying warm. When temperatures drop, body heat can seep out from beneath you, necessitating the use (and weight) of some kind of heat reflector.

The No-Tent Option

There are a few situations in which you might consider hiking without a shelter.

The first is in a reliably dry climate. However, an experience I had in New Mexico sums up the tradeoffs and risks of the no-tent solution, even in a supposedly dry climate. After twenty-something dry-as-dust days and tentless nights, I awoke at about four in the morning on Memorial Day to find a coating of snow on my unprotected sleeping bag. After some grumbling, my little group got up, made breakfast, and started hiking. No harm done. However, it did occur to me that we had narrowly escaped a very uncomfortable night. Had the snow started a couple of hours earlier, we wouldn't have been nearly as cavalier about getting up to start walking. We would have had to do some creative nighttime thinking to rig our ground cloths to hold off the snow. The consequences could have been serious if we didn't have adequate warm clothes and a way to keep dry.

In this case, there was a small but real risk, and we were lucky that the consequences were mere discomfort. The payoff was a lighter pack for many weeks. But I have to say that ever since, I've carried at least an emergency shelter—just in case it happens again.

The second situation in which you might not carry a tent is if you plan to sleep in trailside lean-tos. Lean-tos are found along some popular trails, especially on the East Coast. A trail guide will tell you whether lean-tos are along the trail you plan to hike, and if so, how far apart they are. The problem is, lean-tos are often full during peak hiking season. If a group of six has arrived at a six-person lean-to minutes before you trudge in soaking, cold, and tentless on a rainy evening, you are out of luck. Your only choice may be to walk on to the next one—and hope that it has room for you.

I have known more than one hiker to arrive at a full lean-to and convince the hikers already there to lend a tent. This isn't ultralight camping; it's being a parasite. At the risk of going into school-marm mode, let me say that no one owes you the use of a tent that they have carried on their back. It's also worth noting that while some lean-tos were indeed built in order to allow long-distance hikers to hike without carrying tents, today, the ethic is "first come, first served," no matter who you are. There are too many people on the trails these days to give

Trail lean-tos may eliminate the need for heavy tents, but you'll still want an emergency shelter in case there's no room at the inn.

long-distance hikers priority. In high season, you can expect most lean-tos to be full by late afternoon.

So the first rule for using lean-tos is to have a backup plan, which usually means carrying some sort of minimal shelter: a tarp, a rain fly, or an emergency tent. If you really want lean-to space on a rainy day, plan to stop a little early.

Campsite Selection

Once you've chosen a shelter, good campsite selection can help you maximize its efficiency. With the right campsite doing some of the tent's work for you (blowing away bugs, breaking the wind), you may not need as much from your tent.

As with choosing tents, the first question to ask when choosing a campsite is: What do I need protection from? If you carry a tarp, and you're worried about mosquitoes, you might look for a breezy hill. If you're concerned about a threatening storm and you're above tree line, you might want to head downhill. If you're worried about cold temperatures, you should plan to stay clear of valley floors, where katabatic air currents keep cold air low and close to the ground. If you plan to cook and camp in the same site, you'll need a water source (unless you've carried water). Otherwise, you merely need a flat place (unless you're using a hammock—then, you don't even need that!).

Choosing a soft campsite makes it easier to get a good night's sleep on a thinner, lighter mattress.

Over-Used Campsites

Why do so many people camp in over-used, highly impacted areas? The reasons are numerous. Most hikers like to camp near water, primarily because they tend to stop hiking, set up camp, and then cook their meals at the end of the day. Thus, sites with convenient water access are always at a premium. Also, some national and state parks require campers to stay at pre-established sites. The theory is that it is better to keep using the same sites than to establish a new campsite that is also likely to be overused. But if you are hiking in true wilderness where few others go, or if you are sleeping well away from oft-used camping areas, you can choose to sleep lightly on the ground, making sure that you leave no trace of your camp when you leave in the morning.

The following tips will help you get the most out of your campsite.

▲ When camping in often-used areas, choose obvious sites that have been used before, to concentrate impact. If you are "stealth" camping in a place that looks like it hasn't seen much use, camp out of sight of the trail and be sure you restore the site to its pristine condition in the morning.

▲ Duff and sand both provide good drainage and are soft, which means you'll sleep more comfortably, even on an ultralight mattress pad.

▲ Sites below tree line provide protection from wind and blowing rain. Look for copses of trees.

▲ Above tree line, clumps of bushes and rocks provide protection from the weather, especially if you pay attention to prevailing winds.

▲ For bug protection, look for dry, breezy sites, usually on knolls or at passes. If you are using a tarp, sleep in tightly woven, loose-fitting clothes to provide full body coverage. (Long-distance hikers: These can double as your town clothes.)

▲ For rain and wind protection, pitch the back of your shelter toward the incoming weather. If you're using a tarp, pitch the back end all the way down to the ground on the windward side.

Chapter 4

Oh, for a Good Night's Sleep: Sleeping Bags

Sleeping bags have come a long way since you crawled out of that cotton-stuffed, duck-decorated, sweat-soaked sack at summer camp. Gear in all categories has gotten lighter in the last generation, but sleeping bag design has perhaps dovetailed the most neatly with the lightweight revolution.

Interestingly, the lightest and most compressible fill long favored for high-end sleeping bags is not some fancy polymer cooked up in a chemistry lab. It's nature's own goose down, which offers more warmth per ounce than anything humans have been able to come up with.

Down may indeed be featherweight, but technology is giving nature a run for the money. In the last fifteen years, makers of synthetic fills have taken dramatic steps toward narrowing the performance gap, and today's synthetics, while still marginally heavier than down, offer some advantages that down can't match. You'll find equally experienced hikers making different choices regarding synthetic versus down bags, and many hikers, myself included, have both kinds of sleeping bags in their equipment closets.

Opposite: Getting cozy for the night. (photo by Alan Bauer)

It's difficult to see how the weight of a sleeping bag could be significantly reduced, given that the gossamer fabrics covering the sacks now weigh in at mere ounces. Still, designers keep trying. In addition to the tried-and-true mummy design, innovators have come up with new styles that give lightweight hikers even more choices, including mattress-bag combinations, sleeping coverlets, half-zippered bags, and multi-component sleeping systems that can be adapted to various temperatures.

Sleeping Bag Basics

As with tents, choosing the right sleeping bag begins with a series of questions regarding the conditions in which you plan to hike and (more importantly) sleep. While the primary issues with tents are bugs and rain, the primary concern with sleeping bags is temperature—that is, what is the lowest temperature you expect to routinely encounter?

Don't jump to a conclusion too quickly. Nighttime temperatures can be much lower than you expect. For instance, mountain nights are much colder than those in valleys, so the easily accessible weather forecasts from the airport nearest your destination might be way off base. Another surprise: Desert nights can be startlingly cold—even in midsummer when daytime temperatures hit triple digits.

After you've ascertained the general temperature range, you need to answer a few other questions. Are you planning to hike in a largely dry climate or a rainy one? What kind of a tent will you be using? Will you have a "sleeping partner" (someone with whom to curl up and share a sleeping system)? You should also have a sense of whether you are a warm sleeper or a cold sleeper.

Once you've established these parameters, you are ready to start looking at the designs that might meet your needs.

How a Sleeping Bag Works

A traditional sleeping bag is an approximately human-shaped sac made of an outer layer of fabric containing an inner layer of insulation. This inner layer keeps you warm by trapping warm air from your body and holding it close to you. That's all there is to it.

Sleeping bags are generally described as being "summer bags," "three-season bags," or "winter bags." (Note that there is no such thing as a "four-season bag." As with tents, no single bag can keep you comfortable in all four seasons.) Most hikers begin with a one-temperature-rating-suits-all three-season bag (usually a twenty- or thirty-degree bag). Sometimes, these bags are too warm for summer and too cold for the bookends of spring and fall (They were joking when they said twenty degrees, right?). But if you hike in the typical range of three-season conditions, you'll be able to sleep comfortably most of the time.

A three-season bag is not the only choice. If you will be spending virtually all of your outdoor sleeping time in a temperate forest in the summer, you probably don't need the extra weight and expense of a three-season bag. You may well be more comfortable in a lighter, cheaper summer bag, which typically has less fill and no hood.

Style

Used on major mountaineering expeditions and backpacking trips alike, the mummy bag is the traditional gold standard of sleeping bag design. The mummy bag is shaped to allow just enough room for you inside it. The legs and feet are tapered, and there isn't much space for turning around. A fully zipped, snug, mummy-style sleeping bag does a good job of holding heat in, but if you're a restless sleeper, it might feel about as comfortable as a sausage casing. (On a warm night, make that a steaming-hot sausage.) And some people (especially skinny people) get sore from being forced to sleep in only one or two positions all night long. On the plus side for lightweight hikers, mummy bags provide the best warmth-to-weight ratio.

If you don't like the somewhat claustrophobic mummy design, modified mummy or rectangular bags are available. However, these are proportionately heavier, partly because they use more fabric and partly because, since there is more air to heat, they don't keep you as warm.

If you do choose a mummy bag, be sure it is loose enough for you to at least turn around in (even though this comfort may cost you an ounce or two). If a mummy bag is too tight, your body may push against it and crush or compress the down, which creates cold spots. Note that different bags are cut differently: Some have more room than others, even though they are the same temperature rating. It's worth the time, trouble, and slight feeling of ridiculousness to crawl into a bag in the store and test the fit before you buy.

Some manufacturers have introduced slightly different shapes for men's and women's bags. Women are said to sleep "colder" than men (and hence, to need warmer bags). Women's bags may also be slightly shorter in length, larger around the hips, and smaller at the shoulders. The difference is minimal; again, your best bet is to try it out in the store.

Fill

The ageless question in sleeping bag choices is whether to buy a bag with down or synthetic fill. Traditionally, down has been the lightweight choice, but with today's advanced synthetics, the difference between a down twenty-degree bag and a synthetic twenty-degree bag from the same manufacturer may be as little as a couple of ounces. (Note, however, that design features also affect a bag's temperature rating; more on that below.)

For down, insulating capacity is measured in "fill." Better-quality down has a higher "fill" measurement. Put another way, one ounce of good-quality down fills more space (and hence traps more warm air) than one ounce of a lower-quality down. How much space is what is being measured. An ounce of top-quality down might fill as much as 800 cubic inches of space. Lower-quality down fills far less. A good-quality sleeping bag should have a fill rating of at least 600, preferably higher. Higher-quality down retains its loft longer, including its ability to regain that loft after being squished in a stuff sack all day.

Down is also more compressible than synthetics. This is important for light-weight hikers, who usually carry smaller packs. You are more likely to be able to shove and squeeze a down bag into your micro-capacity ultralight backpack than a synthetic bag.

However, for backpackers, down has one major disadvantage: It loses all its insulating value when wet. A wet synthetic bag, on the other hand, retains some of its insulating value. Thus, traditional wisdom has it that synthetic fill is better for wet climates and down is better for dry climates. (Snow is not as much of an issue, as it can be brushed off without affecting the bag's insulation.) However, I'm not sure this theoretical difference stands up in the field. Having slept through many weeks of truly appalling weather with my down bag, I'm convinced a person would have to be extremely careless or unlucky to get a down bag so wet that it would lose all its insulating ability. As long as you have a reliable tent, and you take standard

GoLite's Feather weighs 2 pounds, 6 ounces and is rated to 20 degrees Fahrenheit. One of its weight-saving features: a short zipper.

precautions such as using a waterproof stuff sack, separating wet gear from dry gear inside the tent, and taking advantage of sunshine breaks to dry out your gear during the day, you shouldn't have a problem, even in very wet weather. The one situation in which synthetic fill is clearly a better choice is if you are hiking in a reliably rainy climate with a tarp instead of a tent.

Many hikers prefer down's compressibility and lighter weight, but it does come at a price: Good-quality down bags are more expensive than synthetic bags. With care, however, a down bag can last well over ten years and many hundreds of nights of backpacking.

The Shell

The fabric that covers the fill is called the shell. Basic shells are a tightly woven nylon taffeta. The tight weave keeps the clumps of fill inside and provides some water repellency.

Unless you plan on sleeping fully exposed to the elements on rainy nights, a waterproof-breathable shell is an unnecessary luxury, both from a weight standpoint and a financial standpoint. However, a water-resistant fabric does make sense, especially if you are using a tarp and a down bag, or if you are taking a lightweight shelter into an iffy environment.

Note that "water-proof" and "water-resistant" don't mean the same thing. A water-proof fabric keeps out water, period. A water-resistant fabric keeps out some water, but not all. For example, if you spill your morning coffee on your sleeping bag, it will probably bead up and dribble down a water-resistant shell. But if you put that same bag outside in a penetrating drizzle, sooner or later the water will soak through to the fill. Water-resistant sleeping bag fabrics are excellent as a line of defense, in case your tent isn't as storm-proof as you thought, or your tarp is pitched the wrong way to the blowing rain. A water-resistant fabric's other advantage is that it is highly breathable, so it lets water vapor from your sweat dissipate. (Note that a waterproof-breathable fabric will also let sweat escape, but in warm, humid weather, it will usually be less breathable than a water-resistant fabric.) Letting sweat dissipate is important because water vapor trapped in the insulation makes the bag heavier and less efficient.

The popular Dryloft is one example of water-resistant sleeping bag fabric. (Dryloft is also windproof, which matters when you are sleeping under a tarp or under the stars.) Microfiber is another water-resistant fabric; it repels water simply through its extremely tight weave. Microfiber is less expensive than Dryloft.

Zippers

The traditional bag has a full-length zipper that runs along one side of the bag; in addition, most bags have foot zippers. Two bags with alternating right-side and left-side zippers of the same gauge can be zipped together for couples.

Zippers are not only heavier than fabric, they also require the use of more fabric and more fill because they must be covered by a "draft tube" (basically, a thin tube of fill that covers and insulates the cold spot created by the zipper). Some manufacturers are experimenting with shortened zippers or no zippers at all. However, in addition to making getting in and out of the bag easier, zippers let you regulate the amount of warmth inside. They also allow you to use the sleeping bag as a coverlet, for one person or two. Further, an open sleeping bag allows you to change position more freely, which can help hikers who experience hip pain and stiffness when sleeping on the ground.

Temperature Ratings

Temperature ratings seem like a simple idea. Supposedly, a twenty-degree bag will keep you comfortable in twenty-degree weather. And so on.

Turns out it isn't nearly that easy.

First of all, one person's definition of comfort is another person's definition of

Two sleeping bags, each weighing about 2 pounds, offer different temperature ratings. Temperature ratings are a function of loft, fill quality, and design.

misery. Second, manufacturers have not been able to agree on a standard. Are we talking comfort or survival? Is the person dressed or undressed? What about the fact that people with different metabolisms sleep differently? That some like it hot, some like it cold? And so on.

If you are comparing bags made by a single manufacturer, the sleeping bag ratings may not tell you precisely how comfortable you will be in that bag at a given temperature, but they will tell you which bags are warmer than others. The challenge comes when you are comparing bags made by different manufacturers. In that case, a basic rule of thumb is that the bag that is loftier is warmer—if and only if the designs are similar. Design features such as hoods, draft tubes, and shape all affect the temperature rating.

In general, it's a good idea to buy a bag that can handle temperatures about ten degrees colder than you routinely expect. This ten-degree buffer will help you deal with the unexpected, plus the inevitable degradation of the temperature rating as the fill compresses with use.

Weight

A fairly direct correlation exists between price and weight: As the first goes up, the second goes down. A three-season bag with a temperature rating of between twenty and thirty degrees can weigh less than two pounds. Any bag in this category is going to be well made as far as basic design fundamentals are concerned (draft tubes, hoods, baffles, etc.). A three-season bag should not weigh more than about two pounds. Several thirty-degree bags are available with manufacturer-stated weights in about the one-and-a-half-pound range.

Lightweight Innovations and Alternatives

Given how light sleeping bags have become, it's unlikely that new designs will mean massive improvements in the warmth-to-weight ratio. So to go lighter than a sleeping bag, you have to look at sleeping bag alternatives.

Sleeping Quilts

Some ultralight hikers have experimented with sleeping quilts, with varying degrees of success. Most of these quilts are homemade, although some specialty companies, such as Nunatak, are making them available commercially. The idea of a sleeping quilt is simple: Insulation keeps you warm if it is on top of you, but if you are lying on it, it's not doing any good. So why carry the weight of extra insulation for the bottom of the bag? The quilt design that seems to work best in the backcountry is one patterned after the innovations of ultralight hiker and writer Ray Jardine. The quilt goes over the body of the person, and a foot pocket at the bottom holds the quilt in place even if the sleeper moves around during the night. However, many hikers have found that this design lets too much warm air seep out the sides. Two solutions have been introduced. Some quilts are sewn to a sleeping bag bottom made of nylon with no insulation; the sleeper is as fully enclosed as he or she would be in a traditional bag, except without any bottom insulation. Other quilts use straps to hold the quilt in place around the sleeper. One example of this kind of quilt is Nunatak's Ghost, which weighs about a pound and is rated for thirty-two degrees. The quilt is tapered to fit the sleeper's shape, a foot pocket keeps it in place, and straps secure it around the sleeping mat.

Adjustable Sleeping Systems

Long-distance hikers whose trips take them through a variety of climatic zones have to address the challenge of staying comfortable in a range of conditions. Several manufacturers now offer adjustable modular sleeping systems as a solution to this problem. The basic idea of adjustable systems is to use layers that can be exchanged or combined for various conditions. The bags have a base layer with one temperature rating and another layer of insulation that can be zipped on. The base bag can be used for typical three-season hiking, the second layer can be used alone in very warm weather, and the two together can be used for colder weather. The zippers involved in these designs can add a lot of weight, so when you evaluate adjustable systems, be sure you do a thorough weight comparison. Unfortunately, designs and styles for these systems are changing so quickly that anything I recommend will probably be out of production and redesigned by the time this book is published.

Elephant Foot and Jacket

This design used to be found among ice climbers, who would sleep in a chest-high "elephant foot" sleeping bag while wearing a down jacket to keep the rest of their torso, neck, shoulders, and arms warm. The theory was that if you are carrying a down jacket anyway, why not make it do double the work? So obviously, this system makes sense only if you are carrying a down jacket—something most three-season hikers don't need. Nunatak makes an elephant-foot bag that weighs about a pound and is rated to twenty degrees. However, with a warmer jacket, it could keep you warm in temperatures down to zero.

For Couples

For years, couples sleeping together have been able to zip their bags together using compatible zippers. Unfortunately, body warmth seeps out at the shoulder and neck areas.

One solution is to use a blanket. A rectangular-cut fleece bag can be unzipped and used as a lightweight coverlet for a couple in warm weather. You might try the same thing with a traditional sleeping bag that has a rectangular shape. (Fleece blankets are bulky and don't have as good a warmth-to-weight ratio as traditional sleeping bags.)

Another solution is a sleeping-bag doubler, such as the Sweetie Pie Sleeping Bag Doubler. The doubler tucks around the shoulders, keeping warm air in. Take the pound-and-a-half doubler and one lightweight sleeping bag, and leave the other sleeping bag at home. Of course, if you're already using sleeping bags that weigh in under two pounds, you won't save much weight. But if your bags are of traditional weight and construction, a doubler will save both weight and money.

Sleeping Mats

A sleeping mat is not just a matter of comfort. It should help you get a good night's sleep, which is more than a mere luxury when you've been hiking all day. The other function of a sleeping mat is to keep you warm: It is part of your nighttime insulation system. The sleeping bag insulates you from above and the sleeping mat insulates you from below. You need protection from both the air *and* the ground. This is true whether you are hiking in the summer or the winter. Any ground that is colder than your body temperature is going to sap heat away from you over the course of a night. If you're cold, you're likely to sleep fitfully, if at all. Indeed, if you find yourself consistently sleeping "cold" despite a twenty-degree sleeping bag and a warm-blooded tent partner, your sleeping pad may not be thick enough to do its job.

All that notwithstanding, most three-season backpackers do not need the thickest, cushiest (and heaviest) air mattresses on the market. How much of a mattress you need depends on your ability to sleep well on a hard surface. It also depends on how well your body retains and produces heat. If you are a "warm" sleeper, you may not need as thick a mattress as people who are "cold" sleepers. A thick air mattress may let you get by with a slightly underweight sleeping bag (and vice versa).

Of course, the longer and thicker the mattress, the more weight in your pack.

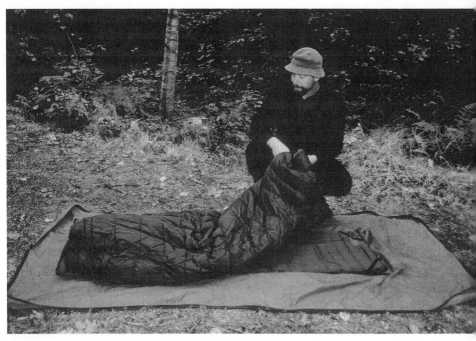

Moonbow's Gearskin placed on a bed of soft forest duff.

At the princess-and-the-pea end of the continuum, full-length mattresses can weigh in at a hefty three pounds. Over on the monkish side are half-length closed-cell foam pads that a self-respecting dog might decline to sleep on. Some extremists leave their mats behind entirely and sleep happily on "beds" made of nothing more than pine duff and leaves. Comfort-obsessed traditionalists may carry an air mattress that feels as soft and cushy as a full-sized bed (well, almost…).

So what kind of sleeping pad do you need?

Air Mattresses

Air mattresses work by trapping your body heat and using it to provide a warm cushion between you and the cold ground. They are warmer, more comfortable, but heavier than closed-cell foam pads. Still, lighter models remain a viable choice for lightweight backpackers. Therm-a-Rest, a popular brand, makes several different styles, ranging from skinny and short to long, fat, and plain old cushy. The lightest—about a pound—are three-quarter-length pads, which provide insulation for your torso, but end somewhere around your thighs.

Many summertime hikers prefer three-quarter-length mattresses because they find that in warm weather, they don't need extra insulation under their legs. Some hikers use internal-frame packs to somewhat cushion their legs from the ground, but this strategy works only if the pack hasn't been out in the rain all day. Other hikers use extra clothes, including raingear (also a dry-weather-only solution). Another strategy is to use a three-quarter-length air mattress for your torso and hips, and a small cut-out of closed-cell foam under your legs. This piece of foam can double as a sitting pad during lunch breaks, especially on cold wet days.

Air mattresses are especially useful on hard ground such as gravel, packed dirt, or on the hard wood floors of trailside shelters. Note that in some state and national parks, you may be required to sleep in designated campsites and may not be allowed to ferret out that ideal bedding site under a grove of soft-needled pine trees.

Murphy's Law, not to mention the laws of probability, dictate that somewhere along the way, someone is going to have a problem with an air mattress. Indeed, air mattresses can and do develop holes from accidental encounters with cactus spines, sharp stones, flying embers, and carelessly misplaced army knives. However, air mattresses are much stronger than they look, and they can be repaired with the glue and repair tape that come with the pad. Duct tape works too. Sometimes, however, a field repair is difficult. Nonetheless, the vast majority of hikers sleep happily on their air mattresses for years (although if the mattresses in my attic are any indication, the vast majority of air mattresses ultimately end up wearing a patch or two).

Closed-Cell Foam Pads

Some people swear by them, others swear at them. I've known tough high-mileage hikers who cheerfully put up with all kinds of inconveniences, but who simply cannot sleep on a thin foam pad and that's all there is to it. On the other hand, some people find foam pads perfectly comfortable. If you sleep easily on a thin air mattress, a closed-cell foam pad is worth a try. (They're inexpensive, and if they don't work for summer camping, you can always use them as an extra pad in the winter.) As with air mattresses, closed-cell foam pads come in various sizes, from full-length to three-quarter-length and shorter. Some hikers cut them down to fit exactly under the torso, with nothing extra. It's also worth noting that in some lightweight backpacks, folded foam pads can be used to stiffen the back of the pack and make a sort of pack frame—an ingenious way to apply the multiple-use principle.

Be aware that in very cold temperatures, you probably need an air mattress—especially if you are feeling cold inside your sleeping bag. Remember that the sleeping pad is only part of your warmth system; if you are cold at night, you should consider a heftier bag *or* a cushier pad.

If you are using an ultrathin minimalist's foam pad with the expectation that you'll find a cozy bed of forest duff and pine needles, make sure that the terrain really offers such soft spots. In the desertlike Southwest, for example, it can take miles of extra walking to find a place to lie down where sharp rocks and stones won't poke you. A thick air mattress may not be the ideal piece of lightweight gear, but you can lay it on a gravel bed and sleep as soundly as a baby. As with so much of lightweight hiking, it is all about choices. Would you rather carry the extra weight all day, or would you rather spend more time at night searching for a comfortable campsite?

Lightweight Sleeping Strategies

Sleeping bags and sleeping mats are only the most obvious parts of the equation whose sum gives you a good night's sleep. Other factors to consider are clothing and site selection.

Clothing

There are three main reasons to wear clothes inside your sleeping bag. The first is warmth. Remember the old wives' tale that says you'll stay warmer if you sleep naked in a sleeping bag than if you wear clothes? It probably didn't make any sense when you first heard it, and guess why? It sounded nonsensical because it *is* nonsensical. If you're cold during the day, what do you do? Put on more clothes. Same is true at night.

In colder weather, wear some sort of wicking long johns and a long-sleeved shirt. You know you've got a well-balanced system when you can sleep comfortably in a pair of long underwear and your sleeping bag. Don't wear so many clothes that you start sweating unbearably. But if you find yourself shivering and unable to sleep, try adding layers, starting with a hat. Don't be tempted to stick your head inside the sleeping bag. Your breath will saturate the insulation with moist air, making it less effective. Instead, draw the bag's hood and neck collar tight around you. If you are really cold, add gloves and/or dry socks in addition to the hat. (Don't wear wet socks at night, hoping they'll dry. They won't, and your feet will stay damp, cold, and uncomfortable.)

The second reason for wearing clothes inside your sleeping bag—even in warm weather—is cleanliness. Imagine not washing the sheets on your bed for half a year. Gross, right? But that's what effectively happens for thru-hikers on six-month hikes. Weekend hikers aren't off the hook, either: Those 40- and 50-mile loop hikes add up. Not only is the dirt unpleasant and smelly, it also can degrade the insulation.

But before you head off to your local Laundromat, consider that washing sleeping bags (especially down bags) also degrades them. Each washing removes some of the oils that contribute to the down's natural insulating abilities. The solution is to keep your sleeping bag as clean as possible. You have two main strategies: Either use a sleeping bag liner or wear clean (or cleanish) clothing to bed.

The third reason for wearing clothing to sleep in is comfort. In warm weather, wearing a layer of clothing to bed may seem counterintuitive. But a lightweight outfit of tightly woven, loose-fitting long pants and a long-sleeved shirt are ideal for warm weather. The fabric provides a barrier between skin and sleeping bag, keeping your bag clean and making you more comfortable. (Let's face it—slippery sleeping bag fabric is not exactly pleasant on a hot humid night.) And the outfit provides plenty of bug protection, so if you're sleeping under a tarp or want to unzip your bag, you don't have to worry about being eaten alive.

Bag Site Selection

Careful site selection is an important lightweight camping skill that can make your sleeping bag and sleeping pad choices work better for you. With careful site selection, you can sleep more comfortably (which means you can get by with a thinner mattress), more warmly (you can use a thinner mattress and a lighter sleeping bag), and without being tormented by bugs (so you may not need mosquito netting).

For a lightweight backpacker, the ideal site is the exact opposite of the campsites you see dotting the backcountry like so many pockmarks. Campsites in areas that are used over and over again become highly compacted, making them uncomfortable because the ground is stripped of its cover and is packed hard. Some sites are so compacted that they actually form hard little depressions. Guess where all the water goes when it rains? That's right—straight under your tent. In extreme cases, I've seen these kinds of sites contain three-inch-deep puddles.

Almost all of the hard, highly impacted sites are near lakes, springs, and streams. Lightweight backpackers often choose to stop near water to cook, and then walk on several more miles to a campsite, taking advantage of the cool, lovely evening hours. This strategy affords enormous flexibility in campsite selection: All you have to find is a place to comfortably lie down.

For comfort, look for sites on pine needles or thick layers of forest duff. Sand is also a comfortable choice. Despite their inviting appearance, meadows tend to be poor choices. The soils can be either wet or hard, and can fill with dew by morning, soaking you and your belongings. (See also Chapter 3, Give Me Shelter: Tents.)

Chapter 5

The Function of Fashion: Clothing

Forget everything the fashion industry would have you believe. Being "cool" in outdoor clothing is all about not being cool. What you want to be is warm. And dry. How you look while you're doing it is beside the point.

Think of clothes as gear rather than fashion and you're headed in the right direction. Like sleeping bags and tents, clothing is all about protection. It's all about keeping body heat in and inclement weather out, helping to ward off bugs, and making you cozy and comfortable at night.

But choosing the right clothing is even more of a personal decision than choosing sleeping bags and tents. Your clothing choices depend on how your body, your hiking style, and your environment interact with one another. (And maybe, just maybe, after you take care of all the important issues, you can consider what colors you like to wear.)

There's no doubt about it, though: Outdoor clothing can be confusing. Perhaps no other category of outdoor gear has changed as dramatically over the last fifteen or twenty years. Wool, silk, and even cotton were once the staples of an outdoor wardrobe, but they have been largely replaced by synthetic fabrics that

Opposite: Function over fashion on the trail. (photo by Alan Bauer)

boast such advanced features as moisture management and antimicrobial coatings. The sheer number of polysyllabic trade names can be daunting. This chapter tries to make sense of it all by looking at some of the most common types of fabrics, describing their functions, and reviewing the different categories of clothing.

If you're a long-distance hiker, take special note of the discussions on layering, which allows you to be flexible through a wide variety of situations. (Even with layering, however, you'll need to exchange your clothes for different or additional ones as the seasons change or your trail enters radically different environments.)

Short-distance hikers who spend most of their time in known territory might pay special attention to the discussion on raingear, which talks about how to get by with less than all-out storm gear.

The Ten-Pound Clothing Bag—NOT!

I once had the opportunity to watch a friend—an inexperienced hiker—pack for a five-day hike. He carefully counted out five pairs of underwear, five pairs of shorts, and five tee shirts. My eyes got bigger and bigger and bigger as I watched him add pound after pound of unnecessary weight to his pack—all for the sake of having a clean change of clothes each day of the hike.

All those attractive ads and glossy magazine covers notwithstanding, no one expects you to look either stylish or clean in the outdoors. To be honest, I'm not sure who the people in some those photos are—certainly none of the hikers I see in the backcountry have perfectly combed hair. And clean clothes? Fuggedaboudit. The hikers I see have trail-worn clothes, wind-whipped hair—and nothing matches. And with the possible exception of gear reviewers for outdoor magazines, no one I know is equipped head-to-toe with clothes that came on the market yesterday.

Face it: Clothing will get dirty when you wear it hiking, and you may as well get used to it. You don't need a change of clothes for every day, or even every other day. Most long-distance hikers carry at most a single change of shorts and one spare tee shirt. Some ultralight hikers carry even less. If you want clean clothes, wash them in camp on a sunny evening.

Once you've abandoned the idea of a different outfit every day, you can address the real issues: What are your actual clothing needs? What do you need to stay warm and dry in cold weather, and comfortable in hot weather? How do you put together a lightweight system that works?

The Law of Layering

Do you remember going outside in winter when you were little? You were probably so bundled up that you looked like (and were about as mobile as) the Michelin Man. As a result, many of us think that the answer to a cold day is a warm— sometimes, a very, very, very warm—outer jacket.

For backpackers, nothing could be further from the truth.

If you've ever tried to hike with one of those over-insulated polar jackets—the kind you could wear ice-fishing in the arctic—you know that it spends most of the day taking up space in your pack because it's too warm to wear hiking. In the evening you might don it for a couple of hours while sitting around camp, but by bedtime, you'll probably abandon it to crawl into your sleeping bag. Maybe you use it as a pillow. Talk about a piece of gear that isn't earning its way—or its weight—in your pack!

The polar jacket is an extreme example, but it makes an important point. Jackets designed for ice-fishing or climbing New Hampshire's infamous Mount Washington in January are not appropriate for hiking—at least, not under normal conditions. When you're working hard hiking all day, you need more control over how warm or cool you are. As outside temperatures rise or fall, or as you work less or more, you need to be able to change the amount of clothing you are wearing—easily—to keep your body temperature at a comfortable level. The way to do this is by layering.

Instead of that polar jacket, imagine that you are carrying several layers of

Since lightweight hikers carry fewer clothes, it's a good idea to wash them and air them in camp periodically.

warm insulating shirts and sweaters. Perhaps in the chill of morning, you put them all on when you crawl out of your sleeping bag. As the day warms and you start hiking, you begin to feel too warm. Off come a couple of layers. When you stop for a snack, you feel a little chilled, so you put a layer back on. And so you continue through the day, making small adjustments to keep yourself comfortable. Sure, you are sometimes carrying extra clothes that you don't need to wear at the moment—but nowhere in your pack is a multipound jacket useful only when the weather is at its coldest. Instead, you have a wardrobe of layers that can be combined in multiple ways to meet various temperatures and weather conditions.

Another, more sophisticated aspect to layering has to do with the function of each layer. Essentially, the clothing nearest your body should be able to wick moisture (sweat) away from your skin and keep it dry. The middle layers of your system should insulate you from the cold. And the outermost layer should protect you from wind, rain, or snow. Selecting the right layers for the right functions is the key to a lightweight clothing system.

About Natural Fabrics

So-called natural fabrics—wool, silk, and cotton—have long been used in outdoor clothing. However, just because a fabric is "natural" does not mean that it is a perfect fit with the natural world. Wool is warm, but bulky, so it takes up too much space in a pack. Silk has an excellent warmth-to-weight ratio, but it absorbs moisture and takes a long time to dry. And cotton is an outdoor disaster. Wet cotton wicks body heat away from your skin so quickly that search-and-rescue people call it "dead man's clothing."

By contrast, today's synthetic fabrics perform the same functions as natural fabrics did, but with fewer disadvantages and less weight. Still, natural fabrics have been around so long that they deserve at least a look-see.

Wool

Of all the natural fabrics, wool is probably the one that has best held its ground against the synthetic upstarts. Indeed, wool has made something of a comeback, particularly merino and cashmere, which are soft, light, durable, and low-bulk, and which don't itch. Wool is commonly used in socks (usually along with a synthetic such as polypropylene for wicking or nylon for durability); it's also used in some sock liners. And of course, if you have an old, beat-up cashmere sweater, it could have a whole new life in your gear closet.

Silk

In the realm of outdoor gear, silk is most commonly used in long underwear and sometimes as a sleeping-bag liner. It feels softer and smoother than synthetic substitutes, and it's warm for its weight, so it provides good insulation. But silk is expensive and it dries slowly—a disadvantage in wet weather.

Cotton

Some hikers prefer the feel of a cotton tee shirt to the feel of polyester, but I suspect this is often a matter of habit, a bias against technology, or ignorance about the alternatives. Certainly, there's no functional reason to prefer cotton. Cotton is "hydrophilic," which means that it loves water. It might feel good in the store, but once you start working, it becomes sweat-soaked and sweat-stained, especially in humid weather. And when cotton is wet—whether from sweat or rain—it takes a long time to dry. Most people find that cotton shorts and underwear absorb too much sweat to be comfortable, especially when the sweat collects under a pressure point such as a hip belt, causing chafing and rashes. Cotton socks are a bad idea for the same reason, even if you are hiking in running shoes. Cotton socks simply absorb too much sweat, and wet feet are prone to blistering.

In warm temperatures, plenty of people hike in cotton tee shirts and even in cotton shorts, with only a bit of discomfort as the price. But in cool temperatures, cotton can be downright dangerous. Typical three-season hiking often involves exposure to spring and fall rains and freezing temperatures. Because water wicks heat away from a human body eight times as fast as air does, wet cotton essentially functions as a heat-sapping device. In cold weather and in exposed windy places, this wet clothing is prone to freezing.

And in winter, the axiom is "Cotton kills." Period. Don't take my word for it—ask any search-and-rescue worker, park ranger, or mountain guide.

Synthetic Fabrics and the Art of Layering

Today, the vast majority of hikers take to the wilderness with clothing made of polymers, fossil fuels, and a host of synthetic materials. These highly engineered products have revolutionized lightweight backpacking, enabling us to be comfortable in colder and wetter temperatures while carrying less weight. Some hikers find it ironic that our supposedly low-impact and environmentally friendly hobby depends on clothing made of fossil fuels and the like. You may not like the idea of them—but you can't beat the performance.

The Under Layer: Wicking Fabrics

The foundation of a layering system is the wicking layer, which is worn next to the skin. Wicking layers sound almost too good to be true. They keep you warm when it's cold, cool when it's warm, and dry when it's wet. And they work.

A wide variety of fabrics is available for wicking layers, so experiment: You might try generic polypropylene, proprietary blends such as CoolMax or Patagonia's silk-weight Capilene, or just plain polyester. One shirt I've used with great success is a simple, inexpensive polyester shirt that looks and feels like a lightweight football jersey. Its salient feature is hundreds of pinpoint holes that let the sweat escape more readily than a shirt with a tighter weave. A shirt like this is easily washed on the trail:

The polyester princess: Synthetics dry faster and don't absorb moisture like cotton does.

It dries in fifteen minutes in the sun. Women might additionally check out some sports bras/top combinations, which have a wicking layer next to the skin.

When selecting wicking layers, take into consideration how much you typically sweat when hiking. People differ tremendously in this regard. Those who are heavy or out of shape sweat more than those who are thin and fit. Muscle mass, acclimatization, and metabolism also come into play. (If you find yourself drinking more water than your hiking partners, you probably produce more water, or sweat, as well.) It's especially important that people who sweat profusely wear a comfortable wicking layer in warm weather.

In moderate or warm weather, a wicking layer—say, a synthetic-fabric tee shirt—can function as the main garment. You don't need insulation in such conditions; quite the contrary, you want your garment to wick sweat away from your body so it can evaporate and keep you cool. (However, garment manufacturers are still limited in what they can do for you. If you insist on trail-running uphill in ninety-degree temperatures, you are going to be uncomfortable no matter what you are wearing.)

In cold weather, a wicking layer is also effective. You may not be aware of it, but you work up a sweat when working out in the cold, and if that sweat stays next to your skin, it can chill you. By wicking the sweat away from your skin, the fabric helps keep you warm. In these cases, you might use a lightweight or midweight, long-sleeved polypropylene or Thermax shirt, which would act as both a wicking layer and an insulating layer. The weight (thickness) you select depends on the temperature in which you plan to be hiking, and whether you will use the shirt while hiking or while resting in camp. Thicker wicking layers are quite warm, and in cool or cold temperatures, many hikers sleep in them. But don't sleep in the layers you wore while hiking—in addition to the cleanliness issue, the sweat will cool and chill you.

Even in subfreezing temperatures, you may find that a lightweight wicking layer is all you need when you are walking. If you get cold, you can always add a vest or a shell. In camp, however, you may prefer a warmer layer. Don't forget the main principles of layering, though. Unless you are hiking in the dead of winter, you'll probably find that two mid- or lightweight layers are more flexible and useful than a single heavy layer.

Finally, when you shop for your wicking layers, take along a postal scale and weigh the clothes before you buy. Weight is not given on clothing labels, and you won't be able to tell the difference between eight ounces and ten ounces without a scale. A couple of ounces may not sound like a lot—but they add up quickly.

The Middle Layer: Insulators

The wicking layer keeps us dry; the middle layer keeps us warm.

Hikers in temperate summer conditions rarely need an insulating layer while hiking, but three-season hikers and above–tree line hikers usually carry at least one insulating layer, and sometimes two.

By far the most popular product for mid-layer insulation is fleece, or, more recently, microfleece (which is, as its name implies, lighter and less bulky). Until very recently, fleece came in a few basic weights (300 was expedition weight, 200 was midweight, and 100 was lightweight); each had an obvious correlation to the warmth it provided. The major differences between the jacket from Company A and the one from Company B were the number of pockets and the colors.

However, in the last few years, gear designers have set their sights on upgrading the technical aspect of this most versatile of clothing—and lightweight hikers are the beneficiaries. In addition to microfleece, today's fleeces may be designed with microfiber (to fit the body more closely), or with layers of windproof material sandwiched in between the fleece.

Fleece or microfleece vests are an excellent choice as part of an insulating system because they hold warmth around your torso (where you most need it) and leave your arms free. You'll especially appreciate a fleece vest when you are wearing raingear. As most hikers know, condensation can be a big problem around the arms. The vest adds warmth to your torso but leaves your arms uncovered, making condensation less of a problem. And, without the sleeves, the garment weighs less, too.

The Outer Layer: Shells

Think of your outer layer, or shell, as your portable tent. Your wicking and insulating layers keep you warm and dry from the inside by managing your body heat and moisture. Your shell protects you from the outside—from the rain, snow, and wind that seek to strip all that warmth away.

In the bad old days, rain protection came in the form of heavy, coated-nylon jackets (think about those heavy yellow slickers deep-sea fishermen are portrayed as wearing). The waterproof coating kept rain out, but it did not allow sweat to escape. Instead, the sweat condensed into droplets coating the inside of the jacket. As a result, if you were doing anything more strenuous than sitting still, you would get wet from the condensation of your own sweat. Worse, those droplets would chill to the ambient temperature,

A full-featured Gore-Tex jacket is necessary in some climates, particularly mountain systems with reputations for storms, but it may not be necessary in a temperate forest.

making them every bit as cold as the rain outside your shell—and you just as wet.

Fortunately, technology has come to the rescue with a plethora of products designed to manage both moisture and evaporation.

Wind Shirts: Wind shirts are light nylon jackets with a tight weave that resists wind but not rain. Although these jackets offer some water repellency, in a heavy rain, they will soak through. However, in windy, slightly damp conditions, they may be all you need. Wind shirts are breathable, and they pack a lot of protection for very little weight. They are especially effective when worn in combination with a fleece jacket and/or a wicking under layer.

Soft-Shell Jackets: Soft-shell jackets are one of the newest categories of clothing to hit outdoor retail shelves. They combine several functions in one: insulating warmth, wind protection, and some waterproofing. They are also breathable, durable, and relatively inexpensive as outdoor gear goes. These jackets are great for colder temperatures when you're more likely to get snow than rain, since snow can be brushed off, whereas rain will ultimately soak through. Three-season hikers, however, may find that combining a wind shirt with a fleece jacket offers more flexibility than having one soft-shell jacket, and may offer enough waterproofing to ward off a brief squall.

Staying Dry: Waterproof Versus Breathable

A loosely woven linen shirt is so breathable that you may not even feel like you're wearing clothing—but get caught in even a light rain and you'll be soaked to the skin in no time flat.

A plastic-coated jacket will keep out the rain, but won't let so much as a drop of sweat escape.

These two extremes illustrate the basic equation that makes staying dry in the rain such a challenge for active outdoorspeople. The more waterproof a fabric is, the less breathable. And vice versa.

Manufacturers have taken a variety of approaches to solving the problem of staying dry in wet weather. Part of the equation, however, depends on the hiker: what climates you hike in and how much your body sweats when working hard.

How Much Waterproofing Do You Need?

It's worth considering how much waterproofing you actually need. Are you likely to experience an all-day downpour? One hiker I know simply refuses to hike in the rain. On a rainy day, he hunkers down in his tent and waits for the weather to change. Since he's a long-distance hiker who has tackled notoriously rainy climates, he carries raingear for those situations in which he may not be able to pitch his tent right away. But since he has no intention of ever hiking all day in the rain, he doesn't bother to carry the most waterproof raingear on the market. For him, a little protection suffices.

On the other hand, having hiked in legendary places such as New Zealand's Milford Sound (said to be the second wettest place in the world, where it once rained twelve inches in forty-eight hours!), the Scottish Highlands, the French Pyrenees, and America's own North Cascades, I can unequivocally say that there are times when you not only want, but *need* raingear that is primarily designed to keep the outside out. The trick is knowing when to carry what kind of protection.

If you are hiking in a temperate region where the weather forecast promises sunshine for days and temperatures in the eighties, do you really need a head-to-toe Gore-Tex suit? The answer is probably not—especially if you have options such as taking shelter in a trailside lean-to, putting up your tent and waiting out the unlikely squall, or shortening your hike by bailing out at a road crossing and checking into a motel. So carrying all the weight of full raingear is not always necessary—or even smart.

If you don't like the idea of leaving all your raingear behind, try carrying a soft-shell jacket, a light poncho, or a wind jacket. All of these offer some rain protection.

Note that any recommendations to skimp on raingear go out the window whenever you are hiking above tree line. Mountains make their own storm systems, and these alpine climates can whip up at least a snow flurry almost any day of the year. The weather can change without notice. Consider where you've seen trees trying to eke out a living: on wind-sheared rocks, through cracks in the pavement, on tenuous footholds through gravel. Trees have a tremendous will to live. If they can't grow someplace, it behooves us humans to take notice.

True, trees usually don't grow at high altitudes because of the fierce winters. But even in summer, the weather above tree line can change without notice, and a natural shelter or easy bail-out point can be rare or nonexistent. Even day hikers on sunny afternoons should carry at least a rain jacket when going above tree line. Hikers who might find themselves many hundreds of feet above the timber need head-to-toe protection, such as a full suit of waterproof-breathable raingear.

Umbrellas

Ask a random group of hikers about umbrellas, and you'll hear them called everything from essential to an utter nuisance. Whether or not to carry an umbrella depends partly on where you're going. If you're traveling off-trail through thick forest or scrambling over rock, an umbrella is nothing but an impediment. On a wide-open, well-maintained trail, however, it could be quite practical. An umbrella can provide effective rain protection when used in combination with a wind shirt or a soft-shell jacket; a side benefit is no ventilation problems. Some hikers use umbrellas as sun protection. GoLite offers a hiking-adapted version of the old standard.

An umbrella offers protection from both blazing sun and buckets of rain.

Ponchos

Ponchos are another solution to the ventilation problem. They are also inexpensive, and a large enough one can ride over a pack as well. Ponchos are not effective in high winds, but you can solve this problem by tying a piece of parachute cord around your waist.

Waterproof-Breathable Laminates

If you've ever been to an outdoor gear fair, you may have seen a Gore-Tex test shower, where you are invited to don raingear and step inside. The point being, of course, that even in a deluge, you will emerge dry inside your protective covering of Gore-Tex.

It's a neat demonstration, but just a tiny bit disingenuous. The conditions inside that shower don't necessarily mimic those faced by a typical hiker, even on the rainiest of days. In order to more accurately reflect a hiker's reality, we'd have to vary the temperature to see if the test worked whether the temperature was thrity-five degrees or eighty-five degrees. And we would also add a treadmill. We'd make

Buying Tips

Price has traditionally been a major barrier to purchasing waterproof-breathable laminate fabrics, but more competition and the introduction of new proprietary fabrics are starting to change that. While you can still spend upwards of $300 for a bombproof, high-end rain jacket, you can also select from a wide range of jackets priced well under $100 (and sometimes less than $50)—all suitable for hiking in milder climates.

Weight has come down as well. Waterproof-breathable rain systems have traditionally been on the heavy side, with the typical pants-and-jacket combo weighing more than two pounds. These days, you should have no trouble keeping the weight of a waterproof-breathable rain jacket well under a pound; in fact, it's not uncommon to find jackets in the ten- to fourteen-ounce category. Plenty of heavy-weights are still on the market, however, so be careful. Look for excess zippers, pockets, and drawstrings, all of which add weight, and carry a postal scale when you go shopping.

Also watch out for imitation products that are not quite as advertised. Some rain suits are advertised as "waterproof and breathable" although they are made of a fabric that is not breathable at all. Manufacturers can get away with this because the design is purportedly breathable: pit zips, venting flaps, and the like supposedly let warm air escape. But a big qualitative difference looms between products that are breathable because of the laminate and products that are breathable because of venting.

One relatively new entry into the waterproof-breathable market is Frogg Toggs' jacket-and-pants set. It has gained widespread popularity among long-distance hikers simply through word of mouth. The set weighs in at less than a pound and costs less than eighty dollars (jacket and pants are also available separately). The design is basic but functional, with a hood but no pockets. The long sleeves can stretch down far enough to cover your hands, but there are no pit zips. The legs have zippers so you can pull the rain pants on over most hiking boots, but the zippers aren't long enough to go over big feet with extra clunky boots. The only serious downside (you knew there had to be one, right?) is that the polypropylene fabric is rather fragile—oddly, it feels a little like a heavy-duty paper towel. And while it's certainly stronger than any paper towel you'll ever encounter, it can be damaged easily by the abrasion of activities such as heavy-duty rock scrambling. Frogg Toggs are sized large, to allow plenty of room for insulating layers and to allow air to circulate inside the jacket.

the hiker climb uphill on it, perhaps while carrying a pack. Chances are that you would not emerge quite as dry from this modified test.

Don't blame the waterproofing. And, no, the jacket didn't suddenly spring a leak. The problem is that while Gore-Tex and similar laminates are both breathable *and* waterproof, they don't work in all conditions.

Gore-Tex and similar products are not actually fabrics. Rather, they are laminates bonded to fabrics. These laminates have microscopic holes big enough to let water vapor escape but too small for water droplets to enter. Waterproof-breathable laminates work best in cool weather, when a significant temperature differential exists between the air inside the jacket and the air outside. When the outside temperature rises, however, most laminates don't perform as well. After water vapor trapped inside the shell condenses, it can't get out. Therefore, if the temperature is even moderately warm, if the humidity is high (if it's raining, there is high humidity), and if you're doing anything more strenuous than munching on a granola bar, your waterproof-breathable shell may not keep you dry, especially if you sweat heavily.

The search for the ultimate in raingear remains frustratingly elusive, a Holy Grail that hovers tantalizingly beyond the reach of technology. What we do have is a variety of options from which to choose. Some waterproof-breathable laminates are more waterproof and less breathable. Others are more breathable, but in an all-day downpour, they may let some water in.

Gore-Tex is merely one of the waterproof-breathable laminates available, albeit the first and the best known. Many outdoor gear companies are making their own, some with interesting twists. Marmot's MemBrain, for example, is said to vary the breathability depending on the temperature. Other manufacturers supplement breathability with design features such as "pit zips" (under the arms) and other strategically placed vents. Another way to reduce condensation is to choose a slightly oversized jacket, which leaves room for both insulating layers and airflow. Finally, most hikers prefer triple-layer Gore-Tex, in which the laminate layer is sandwiched between an inner and outer layer of fabric. Double-layer Gore-Tex is lined with a fabric that too often acts as a condensation trap.

Frogg Toggs' minimalist, waterproof and breathable jacket is inexpensive and light (about 8 ounces). The material is fragile, and the jacket lacks such weight-adding features as pit zips and pockets, but it will keep you warm and dry in a surprise storm.

Durable-Water Repellency (DWR) Coatings

A new rain jacket sheds water like the proverbial duck's back. But after a while, you'll notice that the drops of water don't bead as easily anymore. You may notice water seeping into the fabric. If that fabric is against your skin, it may feel cold and wet.

The problem is not leakage. In fact, if you took that jacket inside the test shower and stood there, you'd come out dry, even though the jacket might look wet from the outside.

The waterproofing, remember, is a function of the laminate. The outer shell of the fabric is not waterproof, but it is treated with a compound known as a DWR coating. This coating wears off over time. To restore it, apply a product such as Nikwax. Ironing the jacket can also help.

Finally, remember that Gore-Tex and similar products need to be kept clean. If dirt clogs up the laminate, the product can't work.

The Rest of the Wardrobe
Shorts Versus Long Pants

Being an outdoor writer I own, of course, an extensive outdoor library. I've just picked up two different books and turned to the chapters on clothing. One writer unreservedly recommends hiking in shorts. The other says he never hikes in shorts. Both advise that you do what they do.

For what it's worth, the vast majority of three-season hikers wear shorts when hiking. Shorts give your legs unrestricted movement and are cooler than long pants. (Hikers with thick or muscular thighs, however, might experience painful chafing when hiking in shorts, especially when going uphill in warm weather. Lycra bicycle-style shorts, minus the bike seat padding, are one solution.)

In some circumstances, however, long pants offer benefits of their own. In poison ivy country, they can save your skin (literally)—although you need to be careful about handling them after you've waded through a poison ivy patch because they will retain the toxic oils until they are washed. Long pants are also a good

Shade clothes—light, nylon long pants and a long-sleeved shirt—keep off sun and bugs.

idea when you're hiking in tick country, under a blazingly fierce sun, or when the mosquitoes are driving you nuts. They'll also protect your skin from getting ripped up when you have to glissade on snow.

What's a lightweight hiker to do?

Convertible shorts with zip-on pant legs are an option that allows you to take both shorts and pants in a single garment. Despite the fact that yet a third writer declares them next to useless, convertible shorts are a fine example of making one piece of gear do two jobs. You should try these on carefully, making sure the zip-on legs are comfortable and the zippers don't chafe. Also look for pant legs with ankle zippers, so you can get the legs on and off over your boots. Long-distance hikers might find the pants more presentable in town; they can also be worn as anti-bug clothing at night and while hiking on cooler days. And they offer yet another solution to the chafing between the legs problem: These shorts generally don't ride up as much (which means the skin stays covered and won't chafe). If you do have a chafing problem, you can always zip on the pant legs.

Camp Clothes

Long pants and long-sleeved shirts are great camp clothes because they serve multiple functions, including fending off evening chill and protecting you from bugs. Look for loose fit and close weaves (so the bugs can't bite through). They also make good sleeping clothes. In colder weather, you may want to wear a wicking layer. In warmer weather, wear looser clothing for comfort. An additional benefit: Your sleeping bag will stay cleaner (prolonging its life). These clothes can be used by long-distance hikers as town clothes as well.

Hats

Hats more than earn their weight in a backpack (or on your head) by protecting you against bugs, sun, cold, rain, and wind.

A wide-brimmed hat shades your neck and face from the sun. A desert-style cap with neck flaps also protects your neck.

A wide-brimmed hat will help keep some insects at bay, although not mosquitoes. The brim seems to interfere with the up-and-down movement of some biting flies. Gnats, which are attracted to the highest part of a person (in a gnat-infested area, try walking with your hand up in the air—you'll see what I mean!) will be attracted to the brim and above. Light colors seem to work best. For added effect, spray some repellent on the *brim* of the hat.

In spring and fall, or anytime above tree line, you need some sort of insulating hat. You've probably read that more heat escapes through your head than any other part of your body. This is because of the high number of blood vessels that bring oxygen to your brain. Microfleece hats are incredibly light and offer good protection, retaining warmth even when wet and drying almost instantly.

BAXTER STATE PARK
CAMPING AT AUTHORIZED
SITES ONLY
WITH RANGER

Balaclavas are also very light, and they cover the neck and part of the face as well as the head.

As with any piece of gear, take your postal scale along when you shop for a hat and choose the lightest one that offers the protection you need.

Gloves

Summer hikers don't usually need gloves, although a thin pair of fleece or polypropylene gloves is always a good idea above tree line. (In an emergency, remember that you can put an extra pair of socks on your hands, or cover your hands with plastic bags.) For colder weather, layered glove systems combine liner mittens with waterproof-breathable shells, but these are rarely needed by three-season hikers. Mittens are warmer than gloves.

Undergarments

Many hikers—male and female—find that going without undergarments is the most comfortable option. If you do use underwear, don't choose cotton: Cotton underwear will absorb sweat, make you feel clammy and miserable, and may cause chafing rashes. Some hiking shorts have built in underwear, and some outdoor manufacturers make underwear specially designed for active sports.

Women should carry at least two pairs of underwear, plus pads, as needed, for use during menstruation. Pads are a huge convenience in the outdoors, offering more latitude with respect to when and where you can change them. With tampons, you might find yourself needing to change one when you're out in the open with nothing but a troop of Boy Scouts in sight (and no rocks or bushes to hide behind).

Women additionally have the option of using sports bras, which are an improvement over traditional bras because the seams are designed to lie flat and the straps won't interfere with your backpack. Some of these can be worn without a tee shirt. With a matching pair of underwear, they can be pressed into service as a bathing suit—something that you wouldn't otherwise carry. Look for bras with wicking inner layers to keep your skin cool and dry.

Opposite: Bike shorts without the padding can prevent chafing of the thighs.

Chapter 6

What's for Dinner? Food and Stoves

As you've no doubt discovered, hikers disagree about many things, from the shelters they sleep in to the type of raingear they carry to environmental politics and trail maintenance. But you won't find much disagreement on the subject of food: At the end of a long day of hiking, food is good, and more is better. (Of course, there's always the exception that proves the rule. I've lately read about an experienced long-distance lightweight hiker who is experimenting with fasting on trails. I'm willing to bet, however, that not too many hikers will be following in those particular footsteps.)

Although almost all hikers agree on the need for good food and plenty of it, that's where the consensus ends. Tastes differ, and so do culinary skills.

This chapter is geared to the needs of hikers who are concerned with both food weight and nutrition. It's no great achievement to get your food weight down if you don't care that most of what you are eating is processed wheat, sugar, and chemicals. It's more difficult to come up with a food strategy that works on the trail and is nutritious, too.

Nutrition is an issue that is particularly important to long-distance hikers. For

Opposite: Pop-can stove set up. (photo by Alan Bauer)

hikers on very short trips, there's little harm in hitting the trail with all the snacks you can carry plus an economy-sized package of instant mashed potatoes or anything else that catches your fancy. But the longer you are out, the more important nutrition becomes.

The problem with writing about nutrition, of course, is that nobody—not even the experts—seems to agree about what's good for you. In the last year alone, I've read magazine articles telling me to eat more bread, and articles telling me that bread causes cancer. I've read that meat is good for me, and that it will lead to an early grave. I've read that organic food will save my body, my soul, and the planet, and I've read that going all natural doesn't make much difference one way or the other.

A U.S. Supreme Court justice once famously said about pornography, "I can't define it, but I know it when I see it." Perhaps the same is true of nutrition: We may not agree about it, we may not be able to define it, but our bodies know when they aren't getting it. In his book, *Beyond Backpacking*, Ray Jardine ponders the high attrition rate of long-distance hikers from their trails—in some cases, more than 80 percent. He asks whether the reason so many hikers start getting physical and mental messages that they want to leave the trail is that their bodies and their subconscious know that home is where the food is. Jardine questions whether nutritional deficiencies might manifest as seemingly non-nutrition–related symptoms such as depression and homesickness.

His theory makes sense. Many long-distance hikers try to subsist on a diet of instant noodles. You may survive on such food, but you probably won't thrive. If you are generally a happy, active, energetic person at home, you should certainly be happy, active, and energetic on the trail. If you find yourself depressed, anxious, and unable to face one more rainy day or one more knee-punishing descent, the problem may not be the rain or the mountain: It may simply be that you are malnourished.

Like everyone else, I have plenty of taste buds and plenty of opinions on the subject of food. But given the rich and deep pool of diverse thinking on this subject, I'd be foolhardy to think I have an answer that's right for everyone. What I can offer is the fruit of a lot of observing—of poking my nose into other hikers cook pots, along with information gleaned from discussions with nutritionists who also happen to be endurance athletes. After all, even if you think you've been eating well in the past, it's always a good idea to smell the coffee in someone else's percolator.

Food Weight

How much your food bag weighs depends on what kinds of foods you choose to carry and how many days you'll be hiking. But how much *should* your food bag weigh? The standard answer is that a typical backpacker using mostly dry, lightweight food will need about two pounds per day in three-season conditions, and as much as two and a half pounds per day in the winter. (The extra half-pound compensates for the calories you burn while hiking and sleeping in the cold. Calories, remember, are a measure of heat.)

The two-pounds-per-day figure is merely an average of what hikers actually use and is not written in stone. People have different metabolisms, and some dedicated lightweight backpackers carry considerably less. I've heard people claim that they carried as little as twelve ounces of food per day for as long as a two-week hike, but I can't believe that they weren't pretty hungry the whole time. If you want to experiment with lowering your food weight, start by lowering the weight of your food to one and three quarter pounds a day and see how that works for you.

Hiking is hard work, and the vast majority of hikers lose weight and/or gain muscle mass on a long hike. My own experience has been that on a long-distance trail, I lose weight no matter what or how much I eat. I even managed to lose weight hiking one summer in France, where I ate restaurant or mountain hut meals almost every night. France, remember, is the capital of cholesterol—the home of a hundred different cheeses and a thousand different wines. Yet even in this culinary paradise, my extra pounds melted like ice cubes in the tropics.

When you are planning your backpacking menus, look for foods with as

Nutrition is an important issue for long-distance hikers. When in towns, try to eat foods that are hard to carry or find and prepare on the trail.

many calories per ounce as possible (fats, for example, pack more calories per ounce than do carbohydrates). Lightweight hiker Glen Van Peski of GVP Gear assumes a base line weight of one and three quarter pounds of food a day, and requires that anything he puts into his pack contains at least 100 calories per ounce. That means he's carrying a minimum of 3200 calories. Studies have shown that long-distance hikers covering 15, 20, or more miles a day consistently use more than this—as much as 4000 or 5000 calories a day. But short-distance hikers who usually cover far fewer miles will probably find the 3200 calories adequate. In fact, many novice hikers actually take more food than they need—and carry those extra pounds through the entire hike, all the way to the trailhead and back to their car.

As with everything you put in your pack, it all boils down to a question of balance. You don't want to carry too much food weight, but you need to take enough calories. Especially on longer hikes, food may not be the best place to try to shave ounces, let alone pounds. Yes, food is one of the heaviest items in your pack. But you need sufficient nourishment to keep walking, not to mention to stay healthy and happy. I know two hikers, one a man in his twenties and the other in his forties, who were diagnosed with severe malnutrition on long trails. One of them had to leave the trail as a result. And this is not unusual. Other people have told similar tales.

It bears repeating: Malnourishment may not manifest itself only as hunger

Water weighs 2 pounds per quart. This is a two-day supply for two people in hot weather: Be sure your pack can comfortably carry the water you need.

and weight loss. It may produce symptoms such as depression and lack of energy. So if you feel down in the dumps, take a good look at your food bag.

Basic Outdoor Food Principles

Food that works in the backcountry must, of necessity, meet certain parameters. A favorite home-cooked meal that always raises your energy and your spirits may not be easy to prepare in the wilderness, so you'll have to come up with alternate recipes that do the job. Let's start by looking at the basic principles of outdoor food, then talk about strategies that can fill your pack with foods that are easy to cook, lightweight, and nutritious.

Nonperishable, Lightweight, and Portable

First things first: If you can't carry the food for several days, it doesn't matter how much you like it. Foods that spoil easily should be the first to cross off your list. These include most watery vegetables and uncooked meats. Note, however, that some foods we traditionally refrigerate don't really require refrigeration, at least in the short term. Sausage, cheese, even hard-boiled eggs will keep for several days—much longer than bread, which we typically don't refrigerate, but which quickly turns moldy, especially in warm, humid climates. Some hikers carry par-boiled eggs (eggs that have been dropped into water for only a few seconds to strengthen the shell), but I think this is one of those things that probably works better in theory than in practice.

Foods that are packed with water (like most fruits and many vegetables) are heavy for their calorie content. They can, however, make refreshing treats. Take less-perishable fruits such as apples and oranges along to eat in the first day or two of your hike.

Vegetables that carry well include cabbage, corn, potatoes, onions, and carrots. Cabbage and carrots can of course be eaten raw; some hikers even eat corn and potatoes raw. (As for onions, you'll have to take that issue up with your hiking partner.)

As far as condiments go, mayonnaise is an obvious thumbs-down, unless you happen to have little sealed packets from a fast-food restaurant. Mustard lasts without refrigeration. So does clarified butter, packets of which are available from some outdoor food outlets. Some hikers carry tubs or squeezable tubes of margarine, but be sure you seal these in double layers of zipper-locking bags.

But by far the foundation of your diet will be dried foods, which don't spoil, pack easily, and are lightweight.

Easily Cooked

Hikers differ in the amount of time they are willing to spend on a backcountry meal. Some hikers travel with exotic ingredients and a full portable cook set complete with spatulas and spice racks. Others just want to boil water and stir. Whichever camp you fall into, you'll want to consider whether your backcountry meal is truly cookable in the outdoors. There's a limit to what you can do with a single backcountry stove, so meals that require par-boiling this and sauteing that are not exactly practical. You'll also want to consider cooking time: Whole grains, for example, often require much longer cooking times than processed instant foods. This presents a problem, because longer cooking times require more fuel, which adds weight to your pack.

No matter how ambitious a cook you are, you'll also need to remember that on some nights you'll be too tired to slave over a hot stove. Or the weather may be throwing a temper tantrum, and all you want to do is curl up inside your tent with a bowl of something hot.

Foods that are easy to cook in the outdoors include commercially packaged mass-market foods available in supermarkets, freeze-dried foods, home-dehydrated foods, and simple recipes, all of which are discussed in more detail below.

Nutritious

Dried foods are convenient and portable, but they present a challenge. Packaged dried foods that are easy to prepare—foods of the just-add-water-and-boil school of cuisine—are often filled with chemicals, preservatives, and flavor enhancers such as monosodium glutamate. They are also typically, if not always, made of highly processed and refined grains such as white rice and bleached wheat—the kind of food that is hardly food at all. If you like that sort of thing and are hiking only a short distance, all is well and good. But for serious hikers, the quality of the food is as important as the quantity of calories. Otherwise, you could just pack a sack full of high-fat, high-sugar donuts and be done with it.

The trick is to find easy-to-prepare foods that are nutritious. Brown grains, for example, have much more nutritional value than processed grains. Whole grains are readily available in food co-ops. Ironically, popular interest in natural foods has grown enough to interest large agri-business, and some products that are now advertised as "all natural" and "whole" may actually be highly processed. Ask at your local health food co-op for suggestions for whole grains and how to prepare them.

Varied

After many thousands of miles of long-distance backpacking, I've decided the answer to the "What's the best kind of food?" question is "There is no single best food." There is, however a "best" food strategy: That strategy is variety. Very few hikers exist on only one kind of food for months on end. Corn pasta went through a brief period of popularity on long-distance trails, because it was touted as a sort of miracle food. The result: Untold pounds of unwanted corn pasta found their way into hiker trade boxes up and down America's long-distance trails. Very few people can happily eat the same food day after day without getting tired of it. Variety can help keep your taste buds happy—and ensure that you get a good balance of vitamins and minerals. If you already have an active lifestyle and you are happy with your current eating program, the best thing you can do is stick as close to that as possible on the trail.

Hot Food Versus Cold Food

Some hikers examine the weight of their stove, pots and fuel, and leap to a seemingly logical conclusion: They'll do without hot food. The late Beverly Hugo, author of *Women and Thruhiking on the Appalachian Trail*, hiked most of the AT without a stove.

But the benefits of this strategy do not necessarily outweigh the liabilities. Very few experienced hikers stick with a cold-food system for long, even if they are interested in lightweight backpacking. Here are some considerations.

Cold food is an option for short weekend hikes.

Weight

First, the weight savings of cold food aren't as great as they first appear. As you'll see below, the weight of your stove and cook gear can be minimized to less than half a pound if you apply draconian lightweight techniques, so leaving a stove at home doesn't necessarily save that much weight. Also, many foods that can be eaten raw have a high moisture content, which makes them weigh more than the types of dried foods hikers usually cook. No doubt a crunchy apple is a treat in the backcountry, but a typical apple contains only 100 calories. For a hiker needing 3000 or more calories a day, apple weight may not make sense.

Spoilage

Foods that are eaten raw (fruits and vegetables) may be more nutritious than packaged dried foods, but they also spoil more readily. In hot weather, they can wilt or rot; in cold weather they can freeze.

Comfort Foods

Hot foods are comfort foods. It simply feels better at the end of a long day to eat a hot meal. (The only exception might be a day spent hiking in a triple-digit heat spell. But those are precisely the conditions that are most likely to spoil any cold food.) I have hiked sans stove on a number of occasions, and I never look forward to a stoveless meal—even a gourmet picnic—with quite as much excitement as a hot meal. If, on those spartan, stoveless hikes, someone had air-dropped me a package of freeze-dried food and a way to cook it, I'd have happily dug in.

Types of Food

Variety is indeed the spice of a hiker's life. The hikers with the most satisfying food bags use a combination of foods from sources ranging from local markets to mail-order suppliers.

Freeze-Dried Foods

Since freeze-dried foods hit the trails a generation ago, they've evolved from simple mac and cheese to fancy offerings like Thai chicken and vegetarian burritos.

The advantages of these meals are obvious: Many are instant, requiring no more than a couple of cups of water and some sitting time. Even the most complicated rarely require more arduous preparation than combining a few ingredients and cooking them for a few minutes. Not all the meals are as tasty as the attractive

A long-distance hiker carefully counts out food for a long stretch.

packaging would have you believe, but many are good indeed, and if you find a few that you like, they add variety and zest to your food bag. Another advantage is their weight. Made especially for backpacking, most freeze-dried meals are lighter than other alternatives. Some, however, are not. Read the packaging and compare weights and portion sizes.

But there are disadvantages. One problem is that freeze-dried meals are often highly processed. Some companies do make foods that they claim contain no artificial ingredients. However, "no artificial ingredients" does not necessarily mean "nutritious." White rice, for example, may not contain any unnatural ingredients, but it has been stripped of its most nutritious elements, leaving a food product with hardly any food value. Processed grains are easier and quicker to rehydrate than whole grains, but at a nutritional cost. Many hikers who rely on a diet of largely freeze-dried foods find that over a long period of time, these foods just don't have enough nutrition and staying power to keep them walking. So if you carry freeze-dried dinners, you might want to compensate by also carrying some whole-grain cereals or breads for other meals.

Freeze-dried foods are also extremely expensive compared to supermarket foods (and even compared to bulk health food store alternatives).

The packaging of freeze-dried foods is both a convenience and a problem. The heavy aluminum packaging keeps the food safe from spoilage and is convenient for rehydrating the meals. But the packaging is not environmentally friendly, it is heavy, and you have to pack it out. Some lightweight hikers repackage freeze-dried meals in zipper-locking bags and rehydrate them in their cook pots.

Supermarket Foods

Packaged foods available in any supermarket are popular backpacking staples. The classic example, of course, is macaroni and cheese. Noodle-and-sauce or rice-and-sauce side dishes, noodle soups, instant soups, instant potatoes, instant rice, and instant oatmeal are all meals that are commonly used by hikers with lightweight food sacks.

Processed packaged mass-market foods find their way into most hikers' packs, but, as with freeze-dried foods, they are difficult to live on and walk on for long periods of time. The more processed the food (white rice, instant oatmeal), the less nutrition it packs. By all means use these packaged foods for your convenience (and budget)—but not exclusively.

Unfortunately, the less processed the food, the more cooking time it requires. There are ways around this problem, though. For example, you can reduce the cooking time (and cooking fuel) of pasta by choosing the thinnest kind available (spaghetti cooks more quickly than linguine; angel hair is better still). With some pastas, instead of following the directions precisely, you can bring the pasta to a boil and let it sit for a while. To cook vegetables very quickly, simply slice them into very thin pieces and drop them in boiling water. Even a potato will be ready to eat in a matter of minutes if sliced thinly enough.

Supermarket foods have the advantage of being cheap and readily available. They also sometimes weigh as little as freeze-dried foods: For instance, a pasta dinner for two made from a half pound of pasta, a can (yes, a can) of tomato paste, and a packet of sauce mix weighs less than two freeze-dried spaghetti dinners. And there's no reason to spend the extra money on freeze-dried mac and cheese. Miniature-sized cans of foods like sardines, salmon, tuna fish, and ham are also available and weigh only two or three ounces. Choose foods packed in oil rather than water to get extra calories without extra weight. You can also add dehydrated vegetables to many pasta meals for added flavor.

Supermarket foods such as cheese, nuts, sausage, crackers, pita bread, bagels, wraps, peanut butter, and jelly make tasty, nutritious, and easy lunches.

Caching water is a good strategy to reduce pack weight and anxiety about finding the next source.

Specialty Foods

One interesting way to vary your hiking diet is to do some of your shopping in ethnic food markets. Prices will vary: If you live in a bonafide ethnic neighborhood, prices will be cheaper than if you live in a yuppie neighborhood, where ethnic food is trendy and expensive. Although noodle soups purchased in an ethnic food store might be no more nutritious than their supermarket counterparts, they can add interesting flavors to your meals. (Not to mention suspense, since sometimes you can't even read the labels!)

Health food stores and co-ops are also good sources of backpacking food. Most contain bins of whole grains—some you've probably never even heard of. Test these first in your own kitchen, as they may take too long to cook, or you may not like the texture or taste. Instant soups are also available in health food stores; they can be both more nutritious and more expensive than their mass-market counterparts.

Some hikers carry beans and soak them in a plastic bowl while hiking. While this is a nutritious strategy, it's not necessarily a lightweight one, since it means carrying an extra pound or so of water.

Home-Dehydrated Foods

Many hikers who take more than a passing interest in nutrition, both in their home lives and during their time on trails, find that home-dehydrating offers the best balance of nutrition, home-cooked taste, and light weight in nonperishable foods.

Dehydrating at home is a relatively simple process, but it's time-consuming to do a lot of it. What takes time is preparing the food, and then packaging it. Dehydrating is most convenient for shorter hikes. Thru-hikers who have tried to dehydrate enough food for an entire six-month trek report that it takes practically as long to dehydrate the food as it does to hike the trail! It's far more practical to make home-dehydrated foods one part of a varied menu, so you don't get overwhelmed. If you want to dehydrate a lot of food for hiking, get a multi-layer dehydrator and cook in big batches. Test-drive your recipes first, though, to be sure of the taste and amount.

Almost any kind of cooked food can be dehydrated. Sauce-based foods like stews and chilis are especially successful as backcountry meals. The book *Dry It, You'll Like It* by Gen MacManiman gives instructions for dehydrating dozens of home-cooked foods.

Snacks

Snacks are a critically important component of a hiker's food plan. You should stop and snack a couple of times a day, to break up steep climbs, give your body a rest, or refuel when you start feeling low on gas.

Energy bars make good hiking snacks, but theories abound as to which bars are best. Some people prefer the high-protein bars, others swear by the high-carb versions. My own theory is that variety is the best approach. I encourage you to experiment. Both health food stores and outdoor retailers carry various kinds of energy bars, but don't forget the inexpensive cereal bars available at grocery stores.

Try supplementing your packaged snack bars with a variety of dried fruits,

---

Mail Order and Internet Suppliers

Mail order and Internet food suppliers go in and out of business so quickly that it's pointless to include contact information in a book. But such companies offer a vast array of foods, including freeze-dried meals, traditionally dehydrated meals, snacks, and bulk dried meats and vegetables—sometimes at deeply discounted prices. A quick Internet search for "hiking food" or "backpacking food" will give you contact information for companies currently in business. You'll also find information about currently operating companies in the classifieds section of outdoor magazines. Also see Resources at the end of this book for some recommended sites and suppliers.

nuts, and dried meats. And if you have a craving, give into it: Most often, your body knows exactly what it needs.

One of the skills of lightweight hiking is to take what you need—but not too much. To calculate how much snack food to take on a hike, plan on taking two snack breaks a day—three if you're doing high mileage. Assume that each snack will consist of either a cereal bar (or two), an energy bar, a handful of GORP, or some nuts. Then do the math. Snack food can be heavy, but its high caloric (and energy) value makes it weight worth carrying.

Cookfires, Stoves, and Cookery

Once you know what kind of food you are planning to eat, you can start thinking about how you're going to cook it and what kind of cooking equipment you'll need. That backpacker's oven might have looked like a really good idea in the store, but are you going to make pizza often enough to justify the extra weight? Do you really need that backcountry espresso maker? Most backpackers try to plan meals that require a minimum of gear and fuel to prepare. One-pot meals are the most popular. This doesn't mean that backpacking should be a monkish ordeal of doing without everything that makes you comfortable. But if you're willing to reconsider and perhaps redefine your idea of comfort, you may find yourself quite happy eating pasta instead of pizza or drinking chai instead of a latte. In fact the added simplicity (not to mention the lighter pack) may even make you more comfortable.

Cook Fires

By far the simplest and most lightweight cooking solution is the old-fashioned cook fire. By cook fire, I'm not talking about a sky-high bonfire. I'm talking about a small, carefully built fire that's just enough to heat your pot. If this idea appeals to you, take into account the following considerations.

Hassle Factor: The nights when you most want and need a hot meal are inevitably the nights when it is most difficult to get a fire going. An emergency fire-starter kit should be part of your gear, but even so, trying to start a fire in a downpour is a pretty miserable way to spend an evening. If you plan to rely on cook fires, be sure you have at least one no-cook meal you can pull out in an emergency. Or be willing to switch your meals around and have lunch for dinner if you can't start a fire or are just too tired.

Regulations: Fires are not permitted in many national and state parks. They are not permitted along the New Jersey and Connecticut sections of the Appalachian Trail. In some wilderness areas, particularly in fragile environments above tree line or in deserts, fires are restricted. And in many places throughout the country, fires are periodically banned during times of high fire danger.

Lack of Firewood: You may not be able to make even a small cook fire if you are camped above tree line.

Environmental Factors: Our constantly dwindling and overpopulated wild areas cannot support unlimited fire-making. Indeed, some popular trails are scarred with the pockmarks of fire-rings left behind by previous campers. Ground cover—and that includes downed and dead logs—functions as habitat for small creatures and as hunting grounds for predators. It also provides nutrients for new growth and soil replenishment. To responsibly make even a small fire, you should ascertain that plenty of downed wood is available, that the area is not overly dried and vulnerable to wildfire, and that you will be able to fully extinguish the fire when you are done and remove all traces of it.

A cook fire should be a small, simple fire made of dry twigs about the size of a pencil, and certainly no wider than a finger. Some minimal-impact outdoor instructors suggest making the cook fire in a small aluminum pie pan, to avoid scarring the ground. (Note, however, that now you have added another piece of gear—the pie pan—to your equipment list.) You can create a wood tripod for hanging your pots over the flames, or use stones as pot supports. (*Warning:* Never use stones from streambeds. They may have absorbed water and can explode in a fire.)

If you are camping in an established site with a fire ring, use the fire ring. If not, don't build a new fire ring. Instead, move flammable duff and pine needles from the site where you want your fire. Build the fire on bare earth, gravel, or sand. In the morning, before you leave, you must ensure that the fire is out. By "out" I mean that you can place a hand on the ground and keep it there. Re-cover the area you burned with the duff and needles you moved the previous night and try to restore the site to how it looked before you got there.

Stoves

Why would you carry the weight of a stove when you can make a fire?

Fires are the ultimate lightweight answer, it's true, but as we've also seen, they do have disadvantages. Stoves offer enormous benefits, especially for hikers trekking in inclement weather. First of all, stoves are (usually) reliable, which means that they *will* light, even if it's cold and rainy and you've had a really tough day. Second, once you get the hang of operating them, they are less fuss and bother than cook fires. Third, they leave no trace. And fourth, they don't blacken your pots and pans the way fires do.

There are dozens of models of lightweight cook stoves, but they basically fall into four categories: gas, canister, alcohol, and wood burning. The first two types are by far the most popular among traditional hikers; the second two are popular among long-distance hikers. To a large degree, the kind of stove you use will be a function of where you're hiking, especially if you hike internationally, where certain types of fuel are more available than others. You will also need to consider how complicated your cooking needs are: Do you just boil water and stir, or do you want to be able to simmer and sauté as well?

Gas Stoves: Gas stoves are the traditionalist's choice. Gas stoves run on white gas, although many of them have now been adapted for multi-fuel use, which means that they can operate on unleaded gas from an auto pump, kerosene, and other fuels. I've even used dry-cleaning fluid (successfully, I might add) when traveling abroad. Gas stoves are the stoves of choice on mountaineering expeditions, and for most hikers who spend a lot of their trekking time at higher altitudes.

The major disadvantage of gas stoves is the weight, which can be upward of a pound. Gas stoves also must be maintained and cleaned periodically or they can be fussy. Some models simmer, some sputter, and some simply roar like a miniature blow torch.

Gas must be carried in a metal fuel container. Some stoves have integrated fuel containers, but these usually are too small to actually carry enough fuel for an entire hike. Fuel bottles come in various sizes. (Smaller ones weigh less, so choose the smallest one for the quantity of fuel you need.)

Pay close attention to how much fuel you actually use when you hike, and take just enough. The fuel containers should be no more than about 80 percent full, to allow the proper pressure.

To operate a gas stove, you must first prime the fuel cup, then, when the cup is hot, you open the fuel jet and—blast off. Or not. Some stoves require in-field maintenance (supplies and instructions provided by the manufacturer). But for the most part, these stoves are reliable.

Canister Stoves: Canister stoves consist of burners that screw into or pop onto

A traditional stove and fuel bottle (front) outweigh a homemade alcohol stove by more than a pound. But beware: Alcohol stoves use more fuel so during long hikes, the difference may dwindle.

a canister containing compressed fuel, usually a combination of butane and propane. These stoves are extremely light, reliable, and can be adjusted to various flame intensities. They are also fuel efficient. But they have their disadvantages. The main problem is that canisters are not recyclable and must be packed out. Also, canisters are not available everywhere, which can be a problem for long-distance hikers or for people traveling to a hiking destination by plane. (You aren't allowed to carry canisters on planes.) Frustratingly, not all canisters work with all stoves, which further complicates matters when you are looking for replacement canisters. The canisters make it difficult to see how much fuel you have left, so until you become good at guessing the fuel level (or unless you make a habit of monitoring your fuel use as you go), you may be stuck carrying an extra back-up canister. Canister stoves don't work well in very cold temperatures (you'll have to sleep with the canister or warm it up inside a jacket), but they do well at altitude because of the lower air pressure. In general, canister stoves offer an excellent weight-to-cooking-time ratio, comparable with even the lightest alcohol stoves (see below).

Combination Fuel Stoves: Some stoves can take both liquid and compressed fuel, although to use both kinds of fuel you would have to carry both the fuel bottle and the canister. These stoves offer flexibility for hikers in remote areas, giving them twice as many opportunities to purchase fuel. However, combination fuel stoves are not especially lightweight.

Wood-Burning Stoves: The Z-Zip stove is a small, wood-burning stove that consists of a burning chamber aerated by a battery-operated fan. With a wood-burning stove such as the Z-Zip, you don't have to carry any fuel—a considerable advantage for the lightweight hiker. On a several-day hike, this can mean losing a pound or more of pack weight right off the bat.

When you come right down to it, however, using one of these gizmos isn't much different from making a small cook fire. You need to have dry tinder on hand, and if rain is threatening, you'll have to collect some pine needles or tiny twigs and carry them for later. And if you're stuck in a forest-drenching downpour for several days, you may have trouble getting your wood-burning stove started at all.

Alcohol Stoves: If you're looking for the lightest stove available, alcohol fuel stoves deserve careful consideration. Alcohol stoves are the most popular choice among serious ultralight hikers. They can be homemade or store-bought.

Alcohol stoves offer several advantages. First, they have no moving parts to break down, and nothing to clean, maintain, or repair. Second, alcohol is an environmentally clean fuel that is readily available at drugstores and hardware stores. Note however, that not just any old alcohol will do the trick. Most alcohol fuel stoves work best with methyl alcohol (methylated spirits or denatured alcohol). Alcohol stoves are considerably less expensive than other stoves, and cost literally pennies if you make your own.

The main disadvantages of alcohol stoves are that they can take seemingly

On the right, a homemade alcohol stove (2 ounces, including pot stand); on the left, Brasslite's 2.5-ounce alcohol stove, complete with pot stand and adjustable windscreen.

endless time to bring water to a boil, and they don't simmer. My homemade alcohol stove takes a full nine minutes at sea level to bring a quart of tap water to a boil. This extended time translates into increased fuel use: Depending on the specific stove, it can take as much as an ounce of alcohol to bring half a quart of water to a boil at sea level. At higher altitudes, it can take twice that much fuel. This is much more fuel than a canister or white gas stove uses. As a result, an alcohol stove is more weight efficient on short trips than on long ones, where the extra fuel weight would cancel out the weight savings of the stove itself. However, you should also consider that you can carry alcohol in lightweight plastic, whereas you have to carry gas in heavy-weight metal.

The Swedish company Trangia makes a classic commercially available alcohol stove set. The lightest model, designed for one person, includes a pot, a handle, the stove unit, and a windscreen, and weighs a remarkable 330 grams (about ten and a half ounces). Fuel, of course, is extra. One advantage of this manufactured stove is that it comes with a lid that can be used to extinguish the flame. (This is important because homemade alcohol stoves can be difficult to "turn off"—a concern in places where fire regulations are strict.)

Some companies weigh in with even lighter systems. Brasslite offers a line of stoves starting at 1.4 ounces. Anti-Gravity Gear's Pepsi Can Stove weighs an almost unbelievable 0.4 ounces, including the windscreen (but not the pot). The manufacturer claims that two cups (about half a liter) of water can be brought to a boil in five minutes using less than one ounce of fuel, and that sixteen ounces of fuel would suffice for an average hiker's five-day trip.

Homemade alcohol stoves are simple to make; the process takes less than half an hour, plus time for the epoxy to cure. Check the Internet (see Resources, at the back of this book) for the most recent designs, but read the safety warnings carefully.

A few cautionary notes about alcohol stoves: Always use the specific type of alcohol recommended by the stove designer or manufacturer. Never cook inside a tent, and never add alcohol to an already hot stove because it can ignite from the heat.

Alcohol stoves are best for hikers whose cooking falls on the simple side of the spectrum. They are also an especially good choice for hikers who cook most of their meals on small cook fires, and who carry stoves for emergencies and rainy days.

Wind Screens and Heat Exchanges: If your stove comes with a windscreen or a heat exchange, use it. Heat exchanges channel the heat around the pot for maximum efficiency. Wind screens keep out the wind and are essential on a blustery day. Both will earn their weight back in fuel conserved.

The Tyranny of Sets

Backcountry cookware can be just as complicated and confusing as any other kind of gear. Often, cook sets come with several sizes of pots and lids, as well as utensils including spatulas and spoons—stuff you probably don't need. When I hike with a partner, our most common configuration is one two-quart (or two-liter) pot, a lid that doubles as a sauté and gravy pan, a pot grabber, and a pot scrubber for clean-up. That's it. Your needs may be different—but just because a cook set comes in an attractive (not to mention heavy...) package doesn't mean that you actually need everything in it.

Pots and Pans: Aluminum is the most popular material for backcountry pots. Titanium is even lighter, but at around fifty dollars a pot, it's too expensive for many hikers. For one person hiking alone, a one-liter pot is adequate. Two people cooking together will be happier with a two-liter pot. Blackening the bottom of your pot makes it retain heat better, reducing cooking time and fuel consumption.

Cups and Bowls: Eating out of the same cook pot is certainly a lightweight strategy, and people do it. But I don't recommend it. Outdoor personal hygiene being what it is, this is a good way to swap diseases. In fact, many experts who have studied waterborne diseases such as giardia believe that more hikers get sick from sharing dirty utensils than from directly ingesting contaminated water. Plus, when you're hungry, you might find that you want your own bowl with your own portion in it. Outdoor stores have a good selection of bowls and spoons. Lexan is a popular material for cups. (A large cup can do double duty as both a cup and a bowl, and if you're hiking solo, it may be all that you need.) Use your postal scale and choose the lightest cups and bowls. Be sure they nest (especially if you hike with a partner): They'll fit more easily in your pack.

Utensils: Think about what's in your food bag, and you'll probably discover that a spoon is the only utensil you need. Some hikers like the fork-spoon combinations, which are essentially spoons with little tines at the edge. Lexan spoons are lightweight and virtually indestructible, despite their flimsy appearance.

Chapter 7

Sweating the Small Stuff

T hese days, outdoor gear retailers are selling scores of things I'm willing to bet you never knew you "needed." Even the most experienced hiker can go into an outdoor store and find a piece of equipment whose use is a complete mystery.

We all like gadgets, but before you pull out the old credit card and tuck away that new toy, it's worth reconsidering for a minute. If you've gotten along without it for all these years, do you really need it?

Do you need a GPS if you are hiking in the middle of summer on a trail that is marked every 100 feet? Do you need a flashlight that can be seen from a mile away? What about that functional but heavy protective case for your maps and guidebooks?

True, some new gear solves problems. The minute you see it, you have that flash of recognition: "Wow! Why didn't someone think of this age ago?" For example, having hiked the Continental Divide Trail before it was largely marked and before the advent of GPS, I was immediately receptive to using a GPS on unmarked trails. It was a no-brainer.

Sometimes the piece of gear is something so elegant and well designed that almost everyone finds it useful—such as a mini-army knife, or the new miniature photon LED flashlights that weigh less than an ounce.

Opposite: Small stuff? Maps and GPS. (photo by Alan Bauer)

But take a moment to make sure a new piece of cool gear really does solve a problem—or else you risk becoming like the heavily burdened day hiker I once met along an easily accessible, well-marked, well-maintained, and well-traveled section of the Appalachian Trail. Despite the ease and accessibility of the trail, this particular day hiker had a heavier pack than many long-distance backpackers. He had an army knife that he could have used to kill a cougar. He had a GPS, a cell phone, *and* a weather radio. He had pouches strapped to both shoulder straps and to his hip belt. His first aid kit could have gotten him through medical school, and his water filter could have cleaned water from the Ganges River. "You never know what might happen out here," he told me in all seriousness.

Well yes, but . . .

If we all prepared for everything that ever could happen, we'd never leave our beds. We'd never take a bath (think of all those slip-and-fall injuries). And we certainly wouldn't leave the house without a suitcase filled with emergency supplies and, quite possibly, an inflatable life-raft. And we would never go on a hike without a fully equipped emergency vehicle following in our footsteps. The truth is, we can't prepare for everything—in life or in backpacking. The trick to choosing outdoor gear is to identify the equipment that will help us best cope with the situations that we expect to encounter and provide a little bit of leeway in case of emergencies. Skills, judgment, and a sensible back-up plan are needed for the rest.

Shaving Ounces

Gadgets and ditties can add a surprising amount to weight to a pack, but some hikers go overboard in the other direction, fanatically seeking and vanquishing those extra ounces with single-minded vengeance. I once watched a hiking partner saw off his toothbrush handle—something that I'd always thought was an apocryphal illustration. He drilled holes into the handle of his spoon, too. Another hiking writer advises people to cut name tags and straps off of their gear.

I don't see any real harm in taking scissors to an unneeded feature, but the weight savings of discarded tags are nothing to write a book about. Do it if it makes you feel good. Do it if it starts getting you in a lightweight frame of mind. But don't expect to turn pounds into ounces by eliminating a few hang-tags. Dealing with especially heavy unneeded features such as a crampon guard or too many extra-long pack straps is probably better considered at the purchasing stage. As we've already seen, there is plenty of lightweight gear now on the market.

More important and far more effective: Evaluate and analyze what you carry, ask yourself whether you truly need it and really use it, and shop for lightweight alternates.

The Ten Essentials

Many years ago, the outdoor and conservation organization The Mountaineers came up with a list of "Ten Essentials"—the ten items that every hiker should carry. It's a good basic emergency kit that has stood the test of time.

Let's look at the list and examine ways to minimize the weight.

Hydration (Extra Water, and a Way to Purify Water)

Reason: Water is essential for survival, even in the short term. You can't be certain that the water sources you expected—from the map or guidebook or hearsay—are really there, and no hiker should risk dehydration.

Weight-saving tips: Weigh water containers and carriers, especially larger ones, before you buy. Use a soda bottle container rather than a heavy-duty backpacker's bottle for carrying your extra water. (Duct tape can hold it together if it cracks). Even on short trips, carry some method for purifying water in case your supply runs out. Iodine tablets are the lightest option, but make sure you don't have a medical condition that precludes their use. On long trips, even if you carry a filter (and/or stove for boiling water), a small container of iodine tablets make a good, lightweight backup system.

How much extra water you carry will depend on the terrain, climate, elevation, water availability, and your own metabolism. On short trips in well-watered

A Nalgene bottle (left) weighs 3 ounces more than a Gatorade bottle (right). However, you can't pour boiling water into a Gatorade bottle.

temperate climates, a quart is usually plenty. On long waterless stretches, hikers doing long mileages sometimes carry more than a gallon.

Nutrition (Extra Food)

Reason: You never know when you might have to stay out a little longer than originally planned. Remember: Food provides the fuel to keep going, to stay warm— and to think clearly.

Weight-saving tips: For extra food choose high-caloric items such as nuts and cheeses. Soup mixes and electrolyte replacement drinks can help replace lost electrolytes and are light to carry and quick to fix. High-calorie energy bars also make good emergency foods.

Insulation (Extra Clothing)

Reason: The weather can change quickly and dramatically, especially in the mountains. Even in warm climates, temperatures drop dramatically when it starts to rain.

Weight-saving tips: It's a good idea to take one more layer than you think you'll routinely need. If your regular clothes get soaking wet, or if the weather takes that dip into record-low territory, you'll be prepared. This extra layer doesn't have to be a full-fledged storm outfit—it can be something as light as a three-ounce wind shirt. In colder climates, take along an extra polypro wicking layer, or a lightweight microfleece vest. Consider the conditions you'll be hiking in, the volatility of the weather, and the exposure. Above tree line, you need a waterproof jacket. Long-distance hikers can make their town clothes do double duty as "extra clothing" for trail emergencies.

Navigation (Map and Compass)

Reason: Getting lost is a drag.

Weight-saving tips: Choose a lightweight plastic compass. A miniature-sized one is adequate on well-marked trails. Cut unneeded sections and margins off maps. (But make sure you don't cut too much of the map away. You may need to know about side trails and roads in case of an emergency, and if you use a GPS, you'll need the grid information.) If you are using a guidebook, photocopy the relevant pages instead of carrying the whole book. Long-distance hikers can put maps and guidebooks for the next section of trail in their resupply boxes.

Fire (Firestarter and Matches/Lighter)

Reason: Whether you carry a stove or not, you should have the means to start a fire. You may need hot food if the weather changes or you are out longer than planned. In an emergency, you may need to start a signal fire. And dry tinder is not always available when you need it.

Weight-saving tips: A several-ounce tube of fire ribbon is overkill. Firestarter

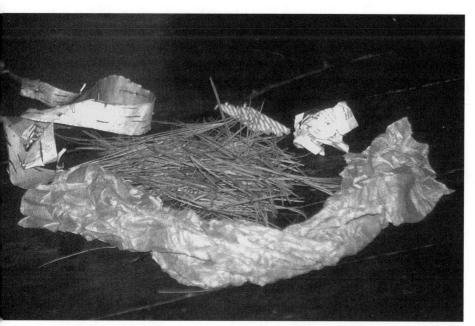

Firestarter can be something you carry or something you find. Clockwise from upper left: birch bark, a few birthday candles, a crumpled-up guidebook page, a Lightload towel made of wood pulp, and, in the center, pine needles.

can be something you already carry, such as cotton swabs (dip them in Vaseline) or old guidebook pages. Birthday candles are also excellent: Drip the wax onto some dry tinder and ignite. You don't have to carry all your firestarter all the time. If bad weather is threatening, pick up bits and pieces of dry tinder as you hike. Look for dry needles and bark (especially pine needles and birch bark, if available). Coat match heads with melted wax to waterproof them, and then store the matches in a watertight plastic bag or a film canister.

Illumination (Headlamp or Flashlight)

Reasons: It may take you longer than you think to get down off that trail. Also, if you plan on bagging some peaks along your hike, you'll need a good flashlight in case you have to start your climb before dawn. (Some climbs start as early as midnight because the snow is stable and mountain weather tends to be more settled at night.) Or, you may be one of those hikers who walk late into the evening and need a flashlight for those last steps into camp. Or perhaps you're an early riser who wants to be up and walking with the first rays of dawn.

Weight-saving tips: Sleek lightweight flashlights are all the rage these days. Some boast beams that can serve as rescue-signaling devices, visible from a mile away; others offer a choice of light colors. Headlamps leave your hands free to

An array of flashlights; note the small item at the far right, a flashlight that weighs only a fraction of an ounce! For night hiking and mountaineering you'll want a full fledged headlamp with a lithium battery. But for finding the privy, a tiny photon is perfectly adequate, while LED flashlights are light and long-lasting.

make or break camp and provide better light for climbing or night hiking. But most exciting for lightweight hikers has been the development of tiny LED lights, which last for thousands of hours, are small enough to clip onto a key ring, provide enough light to read by, and weigh less than an ounce. Small headlamps with several LED bulbs are now available at tremendous weight and size savings. (Note that lithium batteries last longer than standard batteries.)

Repair Kit and Tools (Including Knife)

Reason: Repair kits can hold broken gear together and keep you hiking even if your boots delaminate or your pack frame snaps. A basic repair kit's function is to help you put damaged gear back together until you can get it fixed for real. The repair doesn't have to be elegant; it just has to hold. Contents of a repair kit should include a multipurpose knife; a heavy-duty needle (strong enough to sew carpets); dental floss and/or thread so strong you can't break it with your hands; a finer needle and thread suitable for clothing; about thirty feet of cord (which can be used for lashing things, hanging food bags out of the reach of bears, or drying clothes); safety pins; and the old standby, duct tape.

Weight-saving tips: You don't need to carry a heavy repair kit. Consider the popular multipurpose knives: the more blades, the more ounces. Victorinox and Wenger (the two brands of Swiss Army knives) and Leatherman (the leader in multipurpose tools) have come out with miniature versions that pack multiple tools and blades into tiny packages. Duct tape is now available in small amounts so you don't have to take more than you think you'll need. Or you can simply wrap some around a pen, which has the double benefit of making your pen very visible and easier to find, or hiking poles.

First-Aid Supplies

Reason: People fall, trip, itch, burn, and bleed—and medical help can be a long, long way off.

Weight-saving tips: Your first strategy should be to know what you're doing. First-aid training is more important than first-aid equipment—and it weighs nothing. Second, minimize the contents of store-bought first-aid kits. This is something you'll need to rethink with every trip you take: You'll need to consider how long you're going for and how many people are in your group. Evaluate what you frequently use. Although I always take gauze bandages in my first-aid kit, I only recently realized that never once in 17,000 miles have I ever used one. I still carry gauze bandages—but just one. Minimize the amounts of everything you take, either by buying tiny sample-size portions, or by repackaging small portions into tiny containers.

Sun Protection (Sunglasses and Sunscreen)

Reason: Sunburn and snow blindness are painful, debilitating, and preventable.

Weight-saving tips: Within the realm of reasonable budgets, you can't do much to minimize the weight of sunglasses. (I saw a Titanium pair, but I doubt that even the most dedicated lightweight hiker would consider the ounce or two of weight savings worth the $300 price tag.) Above tree line, you need sunglasses, especially if you will be hiking in snow. Be sure the sunglasses are UV-resistant and have vented side flaps, which block bright light from coming through the sides. The vents help keep the glasses from fogging, too. If your glasses fog when you first put them on, bring them down so that they sit on the edge of your nose for a couple of minutes.

For sunscreen, choose waterproof sunscreen that won't sweat or wash off easily. In buggy conditions, you can double-dip and save weight by purchasing sunscreen with bug repellent. Don't forget that clothing is also an effective sun (and bug) block.

Emergency Shelter

Reason: An emergency shelter can save your life if you have to spend an unexpected night outside.

Weight-saving tips: Backpackers will already have some sort of shelter. But when going into remote areas above tree line, even day hikers (and the most ultralight backpackers) should have some way to shelter themselves. An emergency space blanket or tube-tent weighs only a few ounces. A large, heavy-duty garbage bag can be used as emergency protection against rain and wind.

Beyond the Ten Essentials

In addition to the Ten Essentials, there are a number of other items that many hikers find consistently useful.

Hiking Poles

Hiking poles are like licorice: People seem to either love them or hate them. Their most fervent advocates are hikers who are older or overweight, or who feel a little unsure of their balance or suffer from knee problems. But many younger, fitter hikers are equally enthusiastic.

Poles take stress off of knee and ankle joints on steep downhill stretches, and they aid with balance, especially when you are crossing streams or traveling on scree and talus. I've used double hiking poles for several years, and have found that if I'm hiking on tough terrain (steep boulders to clamber over, lots of stream crossings, and uneven footing), I can outpace and outdistance hikers who would blow past me on easier terrain.

Poles can also help you establish a good uphill rhythm, bringing your arm muscles into play along with your legs. And by giving your hands something to grip and squeeze, they aid in blood circulation, which reduces the edemas that often build in the fingers when you're working and sweating in hot weather.

On the multiple-use front, poles can also be used as tarp supports, and some lightweight tents are designed to be erected with trekking poles as the main supports. Using poles is a great deal easier than finding a conveniently sized stick just lying around.

Get telescoping poles, so they can be adjusted to the desired height. Telescoping poles also can be strapped more conveniently to your pack when you need your hands free for scrambling. It's also easier to travel with telescoping poles when you are going to and from your hiking destination.

As with any gear that becomes quickly popular, trekking poles have spawned dozens of models and styles. Some have springs, which act as mini-shock absorbers, especially on rocky terrain where you have to take big steps. Cork grips are another feature that many hikers like because

Lightload's wood pulp towel weighs 0.5 ounces and takes up about as much space as an Oreo cookie. The disk in the center is the towel in its original packaging.

rubber or plastic grips can actually blister your hands if you sweat a lot—and mosquito repellent can damage them. Some poles come with monopod attachments, to be used with cameras—a clever double-duty adaptation, but one that few hikers need or use.

Garbage Bags

Garbage bags are another multiple-use marvel. They can be used to separate wet gear from dry gear inside a tarp or a tent, or they can be pressed into service as stuff sacks or backpack liners. They can even be used as emergency pack covers or rain/wind shirts. Handle them gently, though, because they tear easily. Grocery bags are another easy-to-find option.

Notebooks

The notes you take on a hiking trip will bring that trip back to life years after the fact. Notebooks don't need to be large and bulky, let alone hardbound. A small notebook is more than adequate, especially for quick trips. Small notebooks with waterproof paper are available in outdoor retailers. Store your notebook in a plastic zipper-locking bag.

Reading Material

Even the most ambitious high-mileage hiker finds that the typical backcountry day involves a lot of time spent hanging around camp, especially in early summer when

On the left, a guidebook (1 pound). On the right, the pages needed for a particular hike (2 ounces). Weight savings: 14 ounces.

the nights are long. What a great opportunity to catch up on your reading (or to become a reader, if you aren't already one). However, the lightweight books (I'm talking here about literary content, not weight) that many hikers carry are a waste of space and ounces because they are quick reads. When you're finished, you have to do something with the book—or else carry it out. (Suggestions: Give it away, use it as firestarter, or leave it in a lean-to where someone else will undoubtedly thank you for it.)

If you're of a literary bent, you might find that backpacking offers a great opportunity to get through those dense difficult books you haven't had time for since college. And a single volume of Shakespeare can last for weeks on the trail.

You can be even more efficient if you're hiking with a partner who has compatible literary tastes. One option is to read a book aloud to each other. Reading aloud takes at least twice as much time as reading to yourself, and you can stop and laugh at the funny parts together or argue about something the author said. If you choose a book of short stories, you can tear and share, allowing both of you to read the same book without worrying about overtaking each other or fighting about who gets to read page 154 first.

Of course, the true ultralight option would be to sit around a campfire and make up your own stories.

Cameras

Unless you are a professional or semiprofessional photographer, a big SLR camera is a liability on the trail. It's big, bulky, and heavy. And let's face it: Expensive electronics and outdoor dirt and weather go together about as well as fish and bicycles.

Small point-and-shoot cameras take 35-millimeter film and produce outstanding

Battery-Operated Things

Most of us carry at least a few battery-operated devices on the trail. Popular items include GPS, flashlights, cell phones, portable radios, and Z-Zip stoves.

By now, you know I'm going to tell you to leave most of these items at home. Do you really need music when the birds are singing? Is the route so difficult or obscure that you need a GPS?

Cell phones can be occasionally useful; they have facilitated rescues and even saved some lives. Women traveling alone might choose to carry cell phones. However, before you carry a cell phone as a rescue tool or safety shield, be aware that it might not work when you need it. In many parts of the country, especially rural or backcountry areas, cell phone service is still nonexistent or spotty; in remote or mountainous areas, you may not be able to get a signal. And remember that the farther out in the backcountry you are, the longer it will take for anyone to reach you. The better plan is to go into the backcountry capable of taking care of yourself, rather than relying on a phone call and other people.

If you do need to carry battery-operated devices, select ones that either use lightweight lithium batteries, or that use the same kind of batteries, so that you don't need to carry several ounces of spares.

images, sometimes suitable for publication. A big advantage for hikers is that these cameras can be easily carried in a front pocket, always at hand's reach (convenient for when you see a bear on the trail). And of course, they are lighter and less expensive than most other cameras. If you frequently travel in rainy weather, you might consider an underwater point-and-shoot camera. If your camera is not waterproof, you need to store it inside a zipper-locking bag inside a case (most camera cases are not waterproof).

Digital cameras are becoming smaller and smaller; the smallest I've seen fits easily in the palm of a hand, and weighs next to nothing. Storage cards for digital cameras can hold varying amounts of photographic information, depending on the quality and resolution of the photos you take. You'll need to calculate how many cards are required to store the number of pictures you usually take. On a long hike, you'll also need to think about how and where you can upload images from your camera to a computer.

Personal Kit

Your personal kit contains your hygiene products: soap, toothbrush and toothpaste, razors, brush or comb, personal medications, toilet paper, nail clippers, and toilet trowel.

Buy sample sizes in drugstores or parcel out your own sample-sized containers. Small plastic travel containers are available at outdoor shops. A small container of liquid soap is convenient for hair, hands, dishes, and the occasional toxic sock that's just too dirty to wear for even one more day. Use a small travel-sized comb or brush for your hair. Check your drugstore for a travel toothbrush that comes with its own toothpaste dispenser. Take a few lengths of sheets off a toilet paper roll (not the whole roll!) and find a lightweight plastic trowel.

The classic multi-use item: A trusty bandana can do everything from mop up a tent to wash a pot.

Chapter 8

Hauling the Lighter Load: The Backpack

Finally, at last, the payoff!

By choosing the right pack, you can lose as much as four or five pounds in one fell swoop—maybe even six pounds, if you swing from a monster-sized load hauler to a svelte little carrier. For most hikers, it's about as much weight as you can lose with a single piece of gear. It's normal to want to start your lightweight hiking career by examining your pack. Why not cut back on the biggest pound-saving equipment right at the start?

Just in case you skipped the introduction and jumped to this chapter with those great weight savings in mind, let me repeat: It's senseless and potentially harmful to try to minimize the weight of your backpack before you've minimized the weight of everything that goes inside it. You wouldn't rent a moving van without knowing how much stuff you intended to move. The same goes for a pack. It's just that simple.

Heavy packs are not built heavily with the intention of weighing you down. There's a method to their apparent madness. Most high-quality, traditional backpacks are loaded with features designed to help you carry a heavier load more

Opposite: Light load or heavy, don't forget the vistas! (photo by Alan Bauer)

comfortably. Problem is, these features (stays, padded shoulder straps, thick hip belts, adjustment straps, and frame sheets) are heavy in themselves. It's a vicious cycle, and the only way to circumvent it is to lighten your load. Only when you have whittled down the mountain of possible gear to a molehill of essentials can you sensibly decide what to carry it all in.

Thinking About Pack Weight

One of the most common mistakes lightweight backpackers make is to think too optimistically about the weight of their load. As explained in Chapter 2, Strategies for a Lighter Load, when lightweight hikers talk about a ten- or a fifteen-pound pack, they are talking about "base pack weight"—the weight of all their gear *not including* the clothes they are wearing, and *not including* food and water. As we've already seen, this convention makes perfect sense, because food and water are always variables. To include them in a discussion about base pack weight only confuses the weight issue.

However, excluding them can make us overly optimistic about how much we are really carrying. Let's take a look at the math: Food and water can vary from five pounds for a weekend (if you're hiking in a well-watered area and don't have to carry much water), to twenty-five pounds or even more (if you're traveling a long stretch in arid country). Add those twenty-five pounds to your "fifteen-pound pack" and you're back at a forty-pound load. Ouch!

Now, this example (extreme though it may be) isn't all bad news. That forty-pound load might well have been a fifty or more if you hadn't gone to the trouble of reducing your base pack weight. Also, that forty-pound load lasts only until you eat lunch and drink your first pint of water. Then it's thirty-nine pounds. And so on.

Still, carrying a thirty- to forty-pound load for a couple of days with a skimpy waist belt, minimal frame, and stripped-down suspension system may not be comfortable for every hiker. You may find that the shoulder straps dig in and your back aches all the time. You may find yourself thinking nostalgic thoughts about the heavyweight features on your old monster-load pack. Or you may find yourself happily skipping along: This is a personal issue, and you'll have to sort out your own balance point between the *amount* of weight you carry and *how* you carry it.

Packweight, Trip Length, and Injuries

With packs as with other gear, short-distance hikers have more latitude than do long-distance hikers. For example, if you are planning a two-week trip with one resupply stop, you could use a lightweight pack. The pack will feel heavy and uncomfortable for the first day or two after you've loaded up with a week's worth of supplies, but that extra food soon gets eaten, and then you have a lighter load. The trade-off may seem well worthwhile, especially because the trip is short and when you go home, your body will have plenty of time to recover.

Long-distance hikers need to be much more cautious because they put enormous strain on their bodies day after day for weeks and months, *without* any recovery time in between. This is a crucial issue, and one that is often ignored. In one study of Appalachian Trail hikers, nearly 20 percent of the aspiring thru-hikers who quit the trail did so because of illness and injury. While leg and foot problems make up the bulk of hiker injuries, strain injuries that affect the shoulders, in particular the rotator cuff, are also common. I've seen hikers suffer debilitating shoulder rotator cuff injuries that forced them to leave the trail, and I myself have had a serious shoulder problem as the result of carrying an improperly balanced lightweight pack. So before you opt for a light pack, be sure you know how much weight your food and water are going to add. If your shoulders consistently ache in more than an "end-of-a-hard-day" sort of way, try rebalancing your load. If that doesn't help, and you will be routinely carrying heavy loads of food and water, you may be better off with a midweight pack, even if your base weight is extremely low. rather than a lightweight pack. Shoulder pain should not be ignored. Such injuries can be severe, and take a long time to heal.

Backpack Styles

Traditional backpacks fall into two major categories: external-frame packs and internal-frame packs. Each category of packs offers an array of sizes and weights, each designed for a different purpose. In addition, there is a third category of new lightweight packs, many of which are variations on the old frameless rucksacks. Rucksacks were traditionally used as daypacks or with very light loads. Today's lightest packs recall that basic design, although many of them have adopted modified load-management features borrowed from their heavier internal-frame cousins.

We'll start by taking a look at traditional packs, then move on to the newer lightweight haulers.

External-Frame Packs

External-frame packs have frames that are visible outside the pack. The sacks that hold your gear are attached to and hung from various parts of the frame, which is usually made of aluminum but sometimes of molded plastic. The frame distributes the weight. An evenly distributed load can't conspire with gravity to pull on your neck and tug on your shoulders.

An external-frame pack tends to keep the center of gravity rather high. Many people find this more comfortable because the weight doesn't pull on the back, neck, and shoulders so much. However, carrying weight high can interfere with balance, especially if the hiker has a low center of gravity. Most women have a lower natural center of gravity, and mountaineers prefer a lower center of gravity when they are dealing with precarious situations. Thus, both groups tend to prefer internal-frame packs, discussed below.

External-frame packs offer additional advantages. They usually have several

pouches and pockets, which are useful for organizing (and finding) your gear. Some external-frame packs have expandable frames, which are convenient for growing adolescents or for people who share equipment with family members or friends. And external-frame packs tend to cost less than internal-frame packs. Most weigh in the four- to five-pound range.

Internal-Frame Packs

Internal-frame packs evolved in the mountaineering world. Essentially, these packs are giant duffel bags with a frame inside. The frame might be a frame sheet (a rigid sheet of plastic that distributes the weight, much as an external frame would); or it may consist of stays (rods, usually made of metal, that are inserted lengthwise into the pack); or it might be some combination of both. It's important that an internal frame pack fit the user's back. Packs come in various torso lengths to facilitate proper fit; in addition, some internal frame packs have stays that must be bent to fit the curve of the hiker's back. (This is usually done in the store when the pack is purchased.)

Because of their close fit, internal-frame packs seem designed to almost hug the body rather than be carried up and apart from it. They are thus better able to move *with* a climber who is bending and twisting.

Internal-frame packs also offer safer stowage: one or two large, duffel-bag style compartments that allow all or most of the gear to be stored *inside* the pack, rather than attached to the outside. Climbers need this kind of storage so their gear can't fall out or off the pack, or snag against rocks or crags. If they slip and fall into a crevasse, they can be sure that everything will stay inside their packs while they scramble out. In contrast, an external-frame pack can get caught on obstructions, and when it does, the sleeping bag or the tent or any other equipment strapped outside might go flying off the mountain never to be seen again.

Internal-frame packs became popular with backpackers who also climbed or scrambled, and/or who liked the lower center of gravity and the tighter fit to the body. They also caught on with international trekkers because they are easier to transport on planes and buses. To meet backpackers' demands, manufacturers of internal-frame packs added external compartments, thickly padded and contoured hip belts, and stays and frame sheets that help distribute the weight and make these packs more comfortable to carry. Load lifters and stabilizers allow hikers to vary the weight distribution between shoulders and hips, and to cinch the load more tightly. The result has been an all-around pack that can handle a heavy load—but that is heavy in itself. Some internal-frame mountaineering and expedition packs weigh as much as seven pounds. (I know one ultralight hiker whose entire base pack weight is less!)

Opposite: Old faithful: The traditional frame backpack has multiple compartments and usually weighs in the 4–5-pound range.

Lightweight Packs

In a sense, backpacks have come full circle. Modern lightweight packs are all about stripped-down function. They are based on the old-time rucksacks ("ruck" is German for back), which were little more than sacks with a few straps. Designers have removed the extra pouches and many of the weight-bearing features that heavier traditional packs use to make their loads ride more comfortably. Lightweight packs make you go back to the basics and reassess what you really need. If you don't have a heavy load, for example, you probably don't need load-lifter straps.

You'll find that lightweight backpacks have stingy features all around. In fact, it's not unusual for an entire light pack to weigh less than the hip belt of an old, monster-load internal-frame pack! A stingy hip belt can be a problem for some women, however, who by and large prefer carrying weight on their hips rather than on their shoulders.

A lightweight convertible pack weighing less than 3 pounds makes a good, inexpensive weekend pack.

Frame sheets and stays are another area where lightweight packs cut ounces, or even pounds, off the total weight. Very light packs do not have frame sheets, and they may have only one stay, or very light stays that are not as sturdy as traditional stays. And needless to say, they certainly don't have external frames.

As a result of these alterations, lightweight packs can either sag (pulling down on your back) or wobble, which feels awkward, interferes with balance, and puts strain on your shoulders, neck, and back. You can, however, devise ways to pack a lightweight load so that it forms a sort of "frame" itself, which stabilizes the pack. We'll take a look at these strategies later in this chapter.

Pack Capacity

First things first, bigger is not better. It is, however, almost always heavier.

Pack manufacturers usually describe pack capacity in terms of cubic inches. Some manufacturers give a range, either because the pack comes in various sizes, or because it has an extension collar. (An extension collar is a piece of nylon at the top of the pack that can be pulled out to expand the pack's capacity for times when you have to haul extra food or clothing.)

As a starting point, let's look at some typical capacity ranges for traditional back-packers. An average weekender on a summer hike might need a pack with a 3500 cubic-inch capacity. A hiker going out for five or six days might use a pack with a 4500 cubic-inch capacity. A winter hiker out for several days in very cold weather might require 6000 cubic inches, while a skilled lightweight backpacker on a five-day hike might be able to manage with 3500 cubic inches or less, depending on the conditions.

Capacity is not only a measure of cubic inches, but also a measure of pounds. If you expect your average fully loaded pack (including food and water) to weigh less than twenty pounds, you may well be comfortable with some of the lightest and simplest packs on the market: those with no frames, no stays, no load lifters, and the most basic hip belts. A stripped down, bare-as-bones ultralight pack may weigh as little as a pound (more usually, two pounds). If your fully loaded pack will weigh more than twenty pounds, you may be more comfortable with a pack that offers some features designed to help you carry the load more comfortably, such as padding on the hip belt, a sternum strap, stays or some sort of frame, and load lifters to adjust the weight from your shoulders to your hips. You should be able to find a pack like this in the three to four pound range. If you typically carry thirty to forty pounds, you will want a pack that uses traditional load-suspension devices. Try to keep the weight of the pack itself less than four and a half pounds.

Packs might also be described as "day packs," "day-and-a-half packs," "weekend packs," "full backpacks," or "expedition packs" (although you should keep in mind that one person's weekend might be another person's expedition). When choosing a pack, consider not only the length of your trips, but also the terrain in which you'll be hiking. Colder, wetter weather and exposed alpine slopes require

Moonbow's Gearskin is a pack-strap system that takes multiple-use to a new level: The pack cloth unfolds to become a ground-cloth or tent bottom. Custom-made systems such as this can weigh in at less than 10 pounds for a two-person tent, ground cloth, pack, and sleeping bag.

more clothes, thus more space in your pack. Longer trips, of course, require more space for food (and a pack that can handle the heavier food weight).

Types of Packs

Day Packs

Day packs are designed to hold gear, food, extra clothing, and water for a full day on the trail. Day hikers' loads can vary widely: Going up a summit above tree line in late autumn, a day hiker needs plenty of warm clothing, good raingear, and the ten essentials (including extra food and water). In contrast, a hiker out for a two-hour romp on a summer trail below tree line might get by with a snack, a pint of water, and little else.

But even when fully loaded, day packs are rarely heavy enough to require much in the way of load-lifting support. Day packs typically do not have frames; some don't have hip belts or sternum straps. However, some hikers prefer these straps and belts, especially for longer hikers.

Day-and-a Half Packs

Day-and-a-half packs are right in line with ultralight thinking. They make serviceable overnight packs, especially for warm, temperate conditions when you need little more than a tarp and a light coverlet. They also can be used for heavy-duty day hikes in challenging terrain, when you want to bring along emergency gear. And they're a good choice for hut-to-hut or inn-to-inn treks, when you don't need to lug all your camping equipment.

Day-and-a-half packs should have some straps on the outside so you can at-

A day-and-a-half pack can carry enough for an overnight in sunny weather, if you pick your equipment carefully.

tach overnight gear, such as your sleeping mattress and possibly your shelter or sleeping bag. (Hint: Use bungee cords to help attach gear more securely, and experiment with attaching your gear before you buy.) However, you can strap only so much stuff to the outside of a small pack. Small packs are not designed for heavy loads dangling off in all directions. I've seen people try this trick on long-distance trails. Without exception, they all sent the packs home and traded up for a pack designed to haul all the stuff they needed.

Standard Backpacks

Although manufacturers differentiate between weekend packs and full-fledged backpacks designed for several days or a week of backpacking in a variety of conditions, not much difference exists between the two, except perhaps a few cubic inches. Whether you're hiking for a weekend or a full week, you need the same basic gear: a stove, a shelter, a sleeping bag, extra clothes. On a weekend trip into high mountains, you will need less food but you might need a warmer bag and more clothing—and your load may be as big as that of a hiker who is going out for a week in a gentler climate.

In general, you want to choose the smallest pack that can accommodate your equipment—and carry it comfortably—regardless of whether the pack is designated for weekends or for longer trips.

Expedition Packs

Expedition packs are designed for loads that very few of us will ever carry. Before you buy one, consider whether you really and truly need it. For the vast majority of three-season hiking scenarios, a hiker who has done even the most basic load-whittling would almost never need to carry more than forty pounds. So why carry the heft and weight of a pack designed to haul twice that? Even long-distance hikers on America's mega-trails rarely carry more than seven days worth of food (fourteen pounds). On the Appalachian Trail, for example, the average hiker resupplies once every four or five days (eight to ten pounds of food). On the Pacific Crest Trail, the average hiker resupplies about every five days.

Unless you are doing a truly unique expedition (exploring the North Pole? Winter hiking in the Tetons? Carrying an entire weekend's worth of gear for a family of six?), you probably do not need an expedition pack. And even if you are going on an expedition, you might not need one of these load-hauling monsters if you've been careful about the weight of the contents of your pack.

Choosing a Pack Size

So how big should your pack be?

When you are discussing pack size with a salesperson, be sure you know whether you are talking about capacity (usually measured in cubic inches) or fit (usually measured as small, medium, or large; may be measured in terms of torso length).

Capacity

One way to determine how much pack capacity you need is to put together all the gear, clothing, and food you expect to take on a typical backpacking trip. If you are going to backpack with it, it goes in the pile. Don't forget your toothpaste, your first-aid kit, your journal, and your camera. If you usually take three-day hikes, pack three days of food. Don't forget your water, extra film, and lucky key chain.

Now, take out the clothes and gear you will wear and use while hiking—your footwear, socks, shorts, tee shirt, and trekking poles. Pack everything else tightly (as you would in a backpack) into a box that is big enough to hold it. When you have found the right box, measure its cubic inches (length times width times height). You now know the approximate capacity of the pack you need. If you don't like the answer, go back through your gear and look for anything you don't need.

Just because your gear all fits in a box doesn't mean it will all fit in your new pack. Sleeping bags, in particular, can be a problem, especially if you are trying to squeeze a noncompressible synthetic sleeping bag into a streamlined ultralight pack. So take that box of gear to the store with you so you can see how your gear and the pack will get along. Before you buy the pack, you need to know what's going to go inside of it as well as how to make it all fit.

Fit

The other aspect of pack size is how the pack fits your body. And be aware that pack size is not the same as clothing size! A tall person, for example, who wears a size "large" doesn't necessarily have a "large" torso size for a backpack. Torso length is measured by taking a tape measure from your neck bone to the small of your back (right between your hipbones). A tall person with long legs may have a medium, or even a small, torso—and vice versa. So be sure you measure your torso length before choosing a size. Some more elaborate (usually heavier, and more expensive) packs also have interchangeable or adjustable components, including hip belts and shoulder straps, and these may also be available in different sizes. Each manufacturer has its own scale.

Pouches and Pockets

Most of us go on several different kinds of trips. This is where pouches and pockets (and bungee cords) come in.

When you're buying your pack, consider how often you might need to carry

Opposite: Modular alternative: Kelty's Cloud weighs about 4 pounds when all its modular compartments and features are utilized and can comfortably carry up to about 40 pounds. The stripped-down version consists of a main compartment and shoulder harness, which weighs just over a pound and is more appropriate for loads under 20 pounds.

more stuff than you've put into that box. If you expect that you'll always hike for three-day weekends in a temperate forest, and you never expect to haul a week's worth of food up a mountain in October, stick with the size you have. One way to make a single pack work for a variety of trips is to choose a pack with multiple expandable components. If you think you might need a larger pack on occasion, consider getting one with an extension collar, optional add-on pouches, or lots of outside lash points. For example, many packs come with detachable hoods. You could choose a pack for your shorter trips that has room in its main compartment for all your gear, and use the hood for extra gear on longer trips.

Kelty's Cloud is an example of a multi-component lightweight pack. Made of long-wearing highly durable Spectra (a fabric that is stronger than steel!), this pack is expensive. It is also completely modular, meaning you can add and subtract pouches and pockets, so the pack works for a variety of load sizes. It's like having three packs in one. The base pack is a central duffel bag with shoulder straps; it weighs in at a pound and a half. You can add a hip belt (highly recommended) as well as several other pouches. Fully expanded, the pack weighs more than four pounds—but it can handle 6500 cubic inches of stuff.

Durability

Of all the gear you use on a backpacking trip, only boots and backpacks take every step with you. Boots and packs are the hardest working pieces of gear in your arsenal, and thus, they are the most subject to trail abuse. Packs may also suffer abusive handling that is not within your control, as, for example, when you are traveling on planes, trucks, or buses, or using alternate, rough, and dirty modes of transportation in developing countries.

One of the ways that lightweight packs cut down on weight is by using lighter fabrics. More expensive packs designed for rougher use may be constructed of a heavy-duty yet lightweight and extremely strong material like Spectra; these are expensive. Packs designed for lighter wear (and lighter budgets) generally sacrifice durability. If you bash through blowdowns and bang on boulders, these packs are going to rip and tear sooner than traditional packs or more expensive packs made of more durable materials. Although an inexpensive lightweight pack can last a thru-hike of a long trail, you can't treat it the same way you can treat a pack made of Cordura. Whenever possible, try to avoid abrading the pack on rocks, dropping it on the ground, or bush-whacking with it. Durability is one of the trade-offs you make with ultralight gear. A repair kit containing a strong needle and carpet-quality thread, some dental floss, and heavy-duty safety pins should be part of your equipment list.

The fragility of some lightweight packs is something to think about when traveling overseas. On the one hand, lightweight packs can make it easier to go on short backpack trips when you're traveling—because you won't be hauling forty pounds of extra gear. But the downside is that, with the exception of the upper-end high-tech packs, most ultralight packs require sometimes delicate handling, which is something to think about if you know you'll have to relinquish it to baggage handlers on buses and trains.

Altering Your Pack

To cut or not to cut: That is a question that has been raised by a new generation of hikers eager to shed ounces. If your backpack features a crampon guard, and you don't own a pair of crampons and have no intention of ever using them, should you cut the darn thing off? What about all those daisy chains and extra straps that you never, ever use?

The easiest answer is that you should avoid buying things you don't need in the first place. Extra features mean more expense and more weight. Plenty of new lightweight packs are designed with minimal features, so you don't have to buy (and carry) more than you need.

But if you have an old pack in your closet that isn't egregiously heavy, you may be able to whittle it down a bit. If you've noticed that you never use certain weight-adding features, it seems ridiculous to lug them around year after year. Pouches, straps, extra lengths of straps, crampon guards, and leather patches, are all candidates for judicious cutting.

Think before you snip, however. One thing to consider is that some pack manufacturers will not honor lifetime warrantees on packs that have been modified. So if you slice your pack to pieces and it falls apart in the field, you can't send it back for a replacement or free repair. Another thing to consider is that the strap you find superfluous today may tomorrow be the strap you need the most. In a flurry of early enthusiasm for lightweight strategies, some hikers cut the hip belts off their packs entirely, and then found that carrying a pack day after day with no hip belt is a sure recipe for aching necks and backs. A hip belt allows hikers to vary the way the weight is divided between shoulders and hips—something you'll appreciate at the end of a long day. (I use a hip belt even if I'm carrying a five-pound daypack; if I leave the hip belt unbuckled, my shoulders and neck start to ache within minutes.) Another item some hikers have removed from their packs, only to regret the decision later, is the sternum strap. Unlike some people, I like using a sternum strap. It doesn't restrict my breathing in the least, and I find that readjusting it during the course of the day helps vary the weight distribution.

So before you snip, consider whether you have successfully used your pack without the feature you plan to cut. Consider the conditions as well. What works on a five-mile-a-day weekend saunter will not necessarily work on a higher-mileage hike with a fully loaded pack, when you might need not only that sternum strap but the load lifter as well.

Packing the Load

Because lightweight packs often have no frames, or very flimsy frames, the load acts as its own frame. Sometimes, frameless packs have a pocket in the back in which you can put your camping mat, which then acts as a sort of a frame sheet. Be sure you try this out in the store, because not all mattresses fit into all packs.

Your pack may come with its own instructions and suggestions for packing. Typically, these will tell you to put your sleeping bag at or near the bottom. However, not all experts agree. Putting your sleeping bag at the bottom means that the entire load in your pack sits on top of it, compressing it. This compression can have a cumulative effect on a down bag. However, with a lightweight load, it's not as much of a problem as with a traditional load.

Pack instructions usually also suggest keeping heavier items up high and close to your back, which distributes the weight more comfortably. This is something you might want to experiment with. Some hikers, especially women and rock-scramblers, prefer a lower center of gravity, in which case, you might try packing your food at the bottom. Whether you pack your heavier items high or low, try to keep them as close to your back as possible.

Most lightweight packs are simply big sacks into which you stuff all your gear (much like the early internal-frame packs). They don't, for instance, have zippered compartments at the bottom for a sleeping bag. So it's important to pack your gear so that you can get at the items you need during the day without having to unpack everything. You'll also want to keep your shelter in a handy place—perhaps even stashed outside the pack—so you can put it up in the rain without exposing your pack and its contents to the weather.

This light Race Adventure pack from GoLite weighs just 1.5 pounds and can handle loads up to 30 pounds.

Waterproofing

Waterproof packs, along with truly waterproof-breathable raingear, are the backpacker's holy grail. Some waterproof packs have been introduced in recent years, but they are even heavier than traditional packs. If you're planning on doing most of your hiking in places where daily rainfall can be measured in buckets, then by all means consider one of these packs. But most lightweight hikers should consider other strategies.

The traditional way to waterproof a pack is to use a pack cover. Rain covers are not an entirely satisfactory solution, since they don't keep 100 percent of the water out, and they tend to collect water down at the bottom of the pack (inconveniently near where most hikers stash their sleeping bags). But for the most part, they keep most of the water out of your pack. They also prevent water from saturating the pack cloth and making it even heavier to carry.

Waterproof stuff sacks are another solution. Stuff sacks made from waterproof-breathable laminates such as Gore-Tex seem somewhat beside the point; after all, your gear doesn't need to breathe! Siliconized nylon stuff sacks weigh far less and do the job; you just have to treat them more carefully in camp. Another choice is to use plastic grocery bags and garbage bags, which have a limited life span, but work especially well for shorter trips.

Sleeping bags and warm clothes need to be protected, if only in garbage bags. Lightweight hiking means making optimal use of the items you do have, and you can't make optimal use of a soaking wet down bag.

Chapter 9

Walking the Walk: Footwear

Why on earth (you may be wondering), have we left boots until the very last? If you've read the introduction, you already know the answer. We leave boots till last for the same reason we left backpacks till almost last. Together, boots and backpacks form the foundation of the entire load-carrying system. If your backpack is the equivalent of your moving van, your boots are your tires and suspension system. You wouldn't put your moving van on tires made for a bicycle; nor can you expect a lightweight boot to carry a heavyweight pack. More to the point, you can't expect your ankles and feet to carry a heavy pack without the support of a heavy boot. The only way to reduce your boot weight is to reduce your pack weight.

And you've done that, right? So let's move on.

A Medical Disclaimer

Advocates of lightweight hiking strategies are not doctors, or orthopedists, or podiatrists. Nor am I. No long-term studies exist to document the impact of hiking long miles with loads on your back (no matter how light). Hiking places

Opposite: Lightweight and versatile hiking shoes. (photo by Alan Bauer)

An ideal trail for running shoes or trekking sandals.

stress on your feet, knees, and ankles, which could ultimately damage your joints and muscles. All we have are personal testimonies—individualistic, opinionated, and subjective.

I have hiked hundreds of miles in sneakers and sports sandals, sometimes successfully, sometimes not. Brian Robinson completed his Triple Crown feat of some 7500 miles in a single calendar year wearing running shoes (he went through several pairs). People have attempted barefoot thru-hikes of long trails. Scores of lightweight backpackers hike in sandals and sneakers. We have no way of knowing whether I—or one of these many others—will some years down the road limp to our local trails with damage traceable to some of this mileage, or whether the fitness and strength we acquired with these activities will keep us limber into old age. Consider that many old-time runners suffer knee and ankle problems from excessive pounding. It seems optimistic to think that hikers are immune.

Just as no one boot fits all hikers, no single footwear strategy is appropriate for everyone. So rather than propose a one-size fits all solution, this chapter will address the various issues and considerations regarding footwear.

It's my job to describe the options. It's your job to apply them to your own particular body. Only you know whether you are a klutz on rock, or whether you float gracefully over obstacles. Only you know whether your ankles are made of marshmallows or iron. There is no single right answer.

Except perhaps, this: Listen to your feet. Listen, especially, to pain messages. They are telling you that something is not right. Do not walk through pain or mask it with painkillers.

If in pain or in doubt, see an orthopedist or a podiatrist. The solution may be something simple, such as using a shoe with a stiffer sole. Or it may be more complicated, like wearing custom-fitted orthodics. Do not rely on someone else's experience to decide what might work for you. If you ask around, you'll find many different experiences and options—some directly contradicting each other. Learn about the options from other hikers—but come to your own conclusions. This is a road you have to walk on your own. Literally. The information in this chapter will provide you with a road map to help you find your way.

Boots as Ankle Chains

An old adage has it that a pound on your feet equals five pounds on your back.

It's one of those things that everyone says, but is there any truth in it? Digging around a little on the Internet, I found disagreement on the details, but not the concept. Various writers and hikers stated that a pound on your feet equals anywhere from three to ten pounds on your back. The only sources mentioned were vague references to a 1953 study of climbers on Everest, and a brief mention of a U.S. Army study. But the number 6.4 kept popping up, and after some more digging, I unearthed a reference to a 1982 London University Human and Applied

Physiology study that concluded that it takes as much effort to move a pound on your feet as it does to carry 6.4 pounds on your back.

The reason has to do with leverage. Specifically, heavy boots work exactly the same way that weights do in a gym. When we attach weights to our ankles in a gym, we're forcing the muscles of the leg to work harder to pick up that weight because it's sitting there all the way at the bottom of our leg. Lifting the same amount of weight strapped to our thighs wouldn't take nearly as much effort, and carrying the same load on our backs would be even easier.

Strapping weights to our ankles makes sense in a gym, where we want to increase resistance and make ourselves work harder. But it makes no sense on the trail, where our goal is exactly the opposite. You would no more hike with ankle weights than you would put rocks in your pack. But effectively, that's what you're doing with heavy-weight boots.

And consider the math: By merely dropping from a four-pound pair of all-leather heavy-duty traditional hiking boots to a light pair of two-pound trekking shoes, we are saving the equivalent of 12.8 pounds.

Getting the Proper Fit

Literally hundreds of trekking shoes and boots are on the market, but most likely you will choose from among only a few, because only a small percentage of them will fit you well. These are the ones you should consider—it doesn't matter how light the others are, or how much you like the features. To paraphrase real estate agents: The three most important issues about choosing a pair of boots are fit, fit, and fit.

But that is not as easy as it sounds.

If you've ever spent any time on long-distance trails, you know that blisters are one of the biggest bugaboos hikers deal with. Neophytes worry about the big-ticket problems like bears and mountain lions; experienced hikers have smaller concerns, like blackflies and blisters.

Good news for lightweight hikers: Lighter, more flexible footwear causes fewer blisters. But they still have to fit—with the socks you're wearing. And they have to fit in the morning, when your feet are fresh, and in the afternoon, after you've hiked fifteen miles and your feet are swollen.

The first thing to look at is basic fit. Have your feet measured on a Brannock device (the name of the shoe-fitting scale you step into). Have your feet measured both sitting and standing. It's best to do this in the afternoon, when your feet tend to be a little swollen. If you have a pair of old boots that fit really well, bring them along for comparison. You should also bring along the socks you intend to wear and any insoles you plan to use.

Opposite: Snow fields can linger well into summer. If your trek calls for miles of snow travel, you'll be happier and safer in boots than in trekking shoes or sneakers.

Your feet should be measured for both length and width, and a good boot or shoe salesperson should know whether each manufacturer's boots run large, small, wide, or narrow. You also want to look at the volume of your foot, which essentially means do you have a dainty ballerina foot or a foot that takes up more space in a boot.

In basic boot fitting, you are checking to be sure there is enough room in the toe box. (Kick something solid: You shouldn't feel your toes against the edge of the boot.) Walk up and down a ramp (you should find one in the shoe departments of any outdoor retailer). Going down the ramp, you shouldn't feel your toes against the boot; going up, you shouldn't feel your heel lifting more than about a quarter of an inch. You should also be able to scrunch your foot forward in the boot and squeeze a finger between your heel and the back of the boot. Finally, check the width: Squashed little toes can cause big-time pain.

If you have had blister and other boot problems in the past, you might want to look for a retailer where the staff have been trained in specialized boot-fitting techniques. Phil Orem's boot-fitting system comes highly recommended by a number of experienced long-distance hikers; you can find a list of retailers who currently offer it in *Backpacker* magazine. This system evaluates such issues as pronation (does your ankle bend inward when you walk), suppination (does the ankle bend outward), protruding bones, and different foot shapes, and recommends solutions such as insoles and padding.

Key blister spots are: back of the heel (easily prevented by putting moleskin on before you even start to hike) and the tops and sides of toes (pare toenails carefully and wrap a sore toe with athletic tape to protect it).

Another foot pain issue is sensitivity, especially foot pain from pounding. This can be a problem with too-light boots under a too-heavy pack. Adding insoles and padded socks can help. So can changing footwear to something with a thicker sole. This kind of pain is more pronounced on hard rocky terrain, and in high heat.

Overall foot fatigue is another issue. Boots hold your feet in a tighter more supportive grip, so even though it takes more effort to move a boot-shod foot, that foot might feel better at the end of a long day. If you feel constant bone and muscle fatigue while wearing shoes, try to lower your pack weight. If that isn't possible, experiment with a lightweight boot.

Types of Footwear
Traditional Boots
Let's start our tour of hiking footwear with a look at traditional boots.

For generations, people took to the backcountry wearing heavy full-grained all-leather boots. The boots weighed a ton (well, okay, maybe about four or five pounds per pair). A foot encased in their viselike grips didn't have much flexibility, but it was protected from everything a trail could put in its path.

I haven't worn really heavy boots for hiking in years, but recently, I found

On the Appalachian Trail's "Rocksylvania," most hikers wear boots for obvious reasons.

myself in a pair of full-fledged mountaineering boots while climbing in Canada's Adamants Range. After the climb, we hiked down off the snow, onto a rocky trailless field. I was rock-hopping too fast, and I momentarily lost my balance. Now, I happen to be blessed with strong ankles, but this time, I landed hard. I could feel my body weight pushing my ankle in a direction it didn't want to go with a force that experience told me was no good. I waited for the pop of pain. And waited. It didn't come: Instead, I felt the boot literally hold my ankle in place and take the force of the jolt for me.

Now, there's no conclusion to this story. I'm not making the point that you need heavy-duty boots. To do so would be to ignore the many valid arguments to the contrary: You could argue that hiking with a lighter boot or a pair of shoes forces a hiker to be more careful. You could suggest that I take ballet lessons or yoga to increase my balance and grace. You could tell me to do ankle-strengthening exercises; or to hike more slowly and carefully. You could remind me that such accidents are rare.

And all of that would be true. My own take on this tale is that it reinforces the concept that different kinds of gear meet different needs. Heavy boots do serve a purpose, and if you are a weak-ankled klutz, they may serve a purpose for you in certain terrain. For most people, however, heavy old-fashioned boots are anomalies. They're simply not necessary on most hiking trails.

Note, however, that for mountaineering and other special uses, heavy boots serve a definite function: Mountaineering boots are designed for warmth and crampons. Winter hikers use heavy leather boots, as do some hikers in extremely rocky and remote terrain. If you are traveling on an expedition to the back of beyond, you want a solid, well-made boot. Then again, most lighter boots last for close to 1000 miles, so even if you are going to inner Mongolia, you might be able to use a lighter boot than the traditional all-leather wafflestomper.

Lightweight Leather

Some manufacturers offer lightweight models of full-leather boots, which weigh in the three-and-a-half-pound range per pair. These boots will typically be cut lower around the ankle, and will be softer and more flexible. Some models are as light in weight as the fabric-leather hybrids discussed below, but they may offer more support.

One advantage to a full-grained leather boot is that leather is fairly waterproof, at least for a while. Once a leather boot gets soaked, it will let in water and your feet will stay wet until the boot has a chance to dry. However, it's worth noting that in leather boots, wet feet are not necessarily cold feet because the leather is good at holding heat in. Wet feet in a leather boot are much more comfortable than wet

Opposite: Before your hike, learn as much as you can about the terrain. Above tree line, scree and talus can challenge unsupported ankles.

feet in a sneaker. Also, in dry weather lightweight leather boots that have gotten soaking wet will dry in a few hours of walking.

Other advantages to all-leather boots include durability: There are fewer seams in a leather boot, which means fewer seams to split. Leather is not nearly as likely to tear as fabric is. And finally, leather boots can also be easily resoled by your local cobbler, something that isn't true for many fabric-and-leather hybrids. You can expect a good pair of all-leather lightweight boots to last for 1000 to 1500 miles; resoling adds more miles to their life span.

One disadvantage of leather boots is that wet leather is heavy; another is that wet feet in wet leather can blister easily. Leather is also less pliable than fabric, so an ill-fitting leather boot is more likely to cause blisters. Good all-leather boots are also more expensive than most fabric-leather hybrids.

Muddy bogs on England's Coast-to-Coast Walk make the author grateful for her choice of a pair of leather-and-fabric hybrid boots plus gaiters.

Fabric-Leather Hybrids

Fabric-leather hybrids are by far the most popular boots on hiking trails. Indeed, they meet the needs of the vast majority of hikers, both those out for short distances and for longer treks. These boots are a compromise, offering the ankle and foot support of a boot with the flexibility and weight of a sneaker (well, almost).

More expensive models come with waterproof-breathable linings. Less-expensive styles are not waterproof—if you step into a puddle past the leather, your feet will get wet—immediately and thoroughly.

The waterproof-breathable lining isn't all it's cracked up to be: These linings usually start to break down within several hundred miles because of abrasion and dirt. However, although the waterproof-breathable lining may not be perfect, it's usually better than nothing. The exception would be in an arid climate, like the American Southwest, where you want total breathability and where waterproofing is almost completely superfluous.

On long-distances hikes, fabric-leather boots tend to break down around the seams. They are difficult if not impossible to resole (and of those that can be resoled, most can't simply be taken to a cobbler, but must be returned to a manufacturer). A fabric-leather hybrid boot usually doesn't last much more than 1000 miles.

Most hikers find that the advantages outweigh the disadvantages. First, and most important, there are dozens of styles, brands, and models to choose from, which means that you're likely to find one that fits. The weight-savings are notable, with these boots weighing in around three pounds. Fabric-leather boots need less breaking-in time than leather boots, and because they are more flexible, blistering is less of a problem. And they are better ventilated than leather boots (although less waterproof).

Hybrids are an especially good choice for traditional backpackers with traditional loads: They offer enough support for a heavier pack, but offer weight savings. They also work well for lightweight backpackers with concerns about balance and ankles, and for those traveling on rocky or muddy terrain.

Trekking Shoes and Running Shoes

In the last ten or fifteen years, wearing trekking shoes and running shoes on long trails has become something of a trend. I first fell into hiking with sneakers by accident in the late 1980s, when I suffered severe blistering in a pair of leather boots. I switched to sneakers and happily hiked for 200 miles in the High Sierra. Since then, I've gone back and forth between sneakers, trekking shoes, and boots, with various degrees of success, and I've watched dozens of other hikers sort out what works for them. What works for most hikers, it turns out, is a variety of footwear. Only a small minority of people hike exclusively in running shoes. The number of people who hike exclusively in boots is decreasing, too, as hikers learn to apply lightweight techniques. A growing number of experienced hikers use different footwear in different conditions.

While there are no hard-and-fast rules, some considerations will help you make a decision about when and whether wearing shoes rather than boots works for you.

Going bootless first and foremost requires that you've gotten your gear weight and pack weight in order. Your total carrying weight for everything should be less than about thirty pounds. To carry more than thirty pounds with only running shoes for support puts you at risk for stress fractures and ankle injuries, particularly on steep terrain.

Choose shoes with good cushioning, especially if you will be hiking on rock. Do not use shoes with air-filled soles; punctures will render them useless.

One problem with running shoes and trekking shoes is that your foot moves around in the shoe more than it would in a boot, where the ankle is held in place. This can lead to problems on rock, where traction is an issue. If your foot is sliding

Southern California's Pacific Crest Trail is a good place to hike in trekking shoes. But in hot terrain, be sure they are roomy enough, as your feet will swell, sometimes a size or more.

around inside the shoe, it may not grip the rock as well. Insoles can be inserted into running shoes to stiffen the support and keep your foot from moving too much.

Be sure the heel cup is fairly inflexible: You need support, or you risk heel spurs and plantar fasciitis, both of which are serious enough and painful enough to derail a hike. If you experience searing heel pain, you may need to take a few days' rest and a course of anti-inflammatory painkillers. Heel-stretching exercises recommended by your doctor or by a physical therapist can give fast relief. You almost undoubtedly need to change your footwear, possibly back to a boot that will hold your heel in place.

When purchasing running shoes or trekking shoes, wear the socks you intend to use. Do not wear cotton socks: They absorb water and hold it next to your feet (which can blister, even in lightweight shoes). Use instead lightweight liners or liners with medium-weight wool socks. Wool socks add a layer of cushioning.

On muddy wet terrain, you will probably be happier with lightweight boots than with shoes. A shoe filled with mud is uncomfortable and exacerbates blister problems. Boot soles also grip better on mud than most shoe soles do.

Be sure the shoe is big enough that your foot has room to swell in it. Many hikers use running or trekking shoes in desert environments, but the heat causes swelling, which can cause blisters if the shoe is too small.

Trekking Sandals

Trekking sandals are recent additions to the trekking shoe category. Sandals first hit the hiking world about fifteen years ago, when hikers started carrying the kind of amphibious sports sandals that were favored by kayakers and rafters.

At first, hikers used these shoes merely as back-up footwear that could be used in camp, in town, and to ford streams. Actually hiking long distances in these sandals was something that only the ultralight fringe was willing to try. Sports sandals lacked cushioning, arch support, and a fit snug enough to provide stability on rocky terrain.

All that has changed with the introduction of new lines of trekking sandals that boast soles with arch supports; bumpers at the front of the foot to protect toes from accidental encounters with rocks and roots, and tighter, more ergonomically designed strapping systems that hold the foot securely in place. Some of the sandals are almost completely open; others are more like a shoe-sandal hybrid, with protective leather around the bottom of the foot, and a more open upper structure.

For lightweight hikers, sandals offer some obvious and attractive advantages beyond mere weight. Sandals are a good choice on gentle trails in dry-ish climates. Some hikers also like them in places with a lot of stream crossing because they can just wade right in without the hassle of taking off boots and socks and then putting them back on every few minutes.

Trekking sandals are usually better suited to gentle trails, but when her heavy leather boots delaminated, the author learned that they could also be used in tough terrain, like here in New Hampshire's rocky White Mountains.

The disadvantages include limited foot support. You'll have to get used to rocks and pebbles rolling around under your feet. Most of the time, you can kick these out or wiggle them out, but sometimes it's annoying to have to stop and address this problem. Sand and small pebbles can cause blistering. You'll also have to step much more carefully, since there is less protection against obstacles ranging from hidden cacti to rocks and roots.

Long-distance hikers who wear sandals without socks (as most people do) may find that over time deep fissures can form in the thick calluses of the foot, especially on the heel (although it's also possible for fissures to form around the ball of the foot). These breaks are caused from a lack of moisture. They can be extremely painful, and are not easily cured in the field. If you find yourself prone to this problem, you might be able to prevent it by putting foot lotion on before bed and wearing a pair of nonwicking socks while you sleep. Wearing waterproof socks with trekking sandals is another approach that has worked for some hikers.

As with trekking shoes, the trekking sandals solution is best for hikers with packs under thirty pounds total weight.

Experimenting

After all my miles of hiking in all different kinds of terrain, I have worn out many pairs of boots with lifetime guarantees. I've tried everything from trekking sandals to running shoes to trekking shoes to hybrids to lightweight leather to full-grained leather to mountaineering boots—and back again. I've switched footwear mid-hike more times than I can count. One some trails I've had blisters, heel spurs, and bone-deep pain. On others, I've had nary a problem. I managed to hike the entire Appalachian Trail without a single blister, while heel spurs almost stopped my Pacific Crest Trail hike cold. I have found that short distance hikes are great places to experiment with a variety of footwear—but that long-distance hikes present their own unique challenges, not all of which can be planned for in advance.

And after all this, all I know for sure is that boots need to fit, they need to be as light as possible, and if they aren't working, I need to change them. There is no one right brand, no one right strategy, no magic bullet. There is only your ever-changing body, the ever-changing conditions in which you hike, and your willingness to experiment with different options to come up with a gear solution that works.

Which seems a good philosophy to end on.

Walk lightly and be well.

Opposite: The author in sneakers on Wyoming's Continental Divide.

Gear–Weight Worksheet for Solo Hikers

Item	Weight "Guesstimate"	Actual Weight	Goal Weight*
Primary Gear			
Boots/Shoes			
Pack			
Trekking poles			
Camping Gear			
Ground cloth			
Mattress pad			
Sleeping bag			
Tent (including poles, stakes, cord)			
Clothing You Wear			
Hat			
Insulating top layer (if necessary)			
Shirt			
Shorts/Pants			
Sock liners			
Socks			
Clothing You Carry (as applicable)			
Down parka			
Extra clothing			
Extra socks			
Gloves			
Insulating pants			
Jacket			
Polypro long-underwear bottom			
Polypro long-underwear top			
Vest			
Cooking/Eating Gear			
Bowl/Plate			
Fuel bottle, canister, or fuel tablets			
Matches/Cigarette lighter			
Pot grabber			
Pot scrubber			
Pot/Lid			
Spatula/Cooking spoon (optional)			

Item	Weight "Guesstimate"	Actual Weight	Goal Weight*
Cooking/Eating Gear (continued)			
Stove (including pump)			
Stove accessories (windscreen, heat exchange)			
Utensil(s)			
Water/Drinking Equipment			
Cup			
Water bottle(s)			
Water carrier			
Water filter			
Personal/Miscellaneous			
Camera/Film			
Camp shoes			
Compass			
First-aid kit (including blister treatment, personal medications)			
Flashlight			
GPS			
Insect repellent			
Journal, pen, notebooks			
Lip balm			
Map/Guidebook			
Pack rain-cover			
Repair kit			
Rope/Cord (extra)			
Sunscreen			
Wash kit (including toothbrush/ paste, biodegradable soap, razor, comb, women's sanitary supplies, toilet paper/trowel)			

Other items _____

_____

_____

_____

TOTAL Gear-Weight _____

* Fill in the "goal weight" after reading this book and determining the specific conditions of your hike.

Gear-Weight Worksheet for Partnered Hikers

Item	Weight "Guesstimate"	Actual Weight	Goal Weight*
Individual's Gear:			
Primary Gear			
Boots/Shoes			
Pack			
Trekking poles			
Camping/Personal Gear			
Bowl/Plate			
Camp shoes			
Cup			
Journal, pen, notebooks			
Lip balm			
Mattress pad			
Pack rain-cover			
Sleeping bag			
Utensil(s)			
Wash kit (including toothbrush/ paste, biodegradable soap, razor, comb, women's sanitary supplies, toilet paper/trowel)			
Water bottle(s)			
Clothing You Wear			
Hat			
Insulating top layer (if necessary)			
Shirt			
Shorts/Pants			
Sock liners			
Socks			
Clothing You Carry (as applicable)			
Down parka			
Extra clothing			
Extra socks			
Gloves			
Insulating pants			
Jacket			
Polypro long-underwear bottom			
Polypro long-underwear top			
Vest			

Item	Weight "Guesstimate"	Actual Weight	Goal Weight*
Shared Gear:*			
Camping/Personal Gear			
Camera/Film			
Compass			
First-aid kit (including blister treatment, personal medications)			
Flashlight			
GPS			
Ground cloth			
Insect repellent			
Map/Guidebook			
Repair kit			
Rope/Cord (extra)			
Sunscreen			
Tent (including poles, stakes, cord)			
Cooking/Eating Gear			
Fuel bottle, canister, or fuel tablets			
Matches/Cigarette lighter			
Pot/Lid			
Pot grabber			
Pot scrubber			
Spatula/Cooking spoon (optional)			
Stove (including pump)			
Stove accessories (windscreen, heat exchange)			
Water/Drinking Equipment			
Water carrier			
Water filter			

Other items _____

_____

_____

TOTAL Personal _____

TOTAL Shared _____

TOTAL Gear–Weight ‡ _____

* Fill in the "goal weight" after reading this book and determining the specific conditions of your hike.
** Weight should be divided by two, or however you typically share the load with your partner.
‡ Personal gear, plus your portion of shared gear–weight.

Resources

Books

There are literally dozens of how-to hiking guides on the market, many of which are excellent. The following two titles, however, are specifically relevant for lightweight hikers.

Beyond Backpacking: Ray Jardine's Guide to Lightweight Hiking, by Ray Jardine. This is an updated and modified edition of guru Jardine's *Pacific Crest Trail Hiker's Companion* and describes his ideas about ultralight hiking. While the newer edition has been edited to appeal to a general audience, its primary interest is long-distance backpacking with ultralight loads. Also see Jardine's website, www.ray-way.com, for information on making your own tarp-tents and other gear.

The Complete Walker IV, by Colin Fletcher and Chip Rawlins. This updated tome is the first stop for any backpacker, lightweight or not. The authors cover the gamut of hiking equipment and skills, providing all the information you need to make choices about technique and load carrying.

Websites

www.backcountry.net: E-lists for those interested in long-distance trails.

www.backpacking.net: Up-to-date gear reviews, community forums, and one of the most complete indexes of manufacturer's websites available. A good place to research new lightweight gear.

www.backpackinglight.com: You must subscribe to use most of the pages here on technique, gear reviews, editorials, gear shop, and forums. Lots of detail and no advertising make it worthwhile.

www.onelist.com/subscribe.cgi/BackpackingLight: E-lists for those interested in lightweight hiking.

www.thru-hiker.com: As the name implies, this site is for long-distance hikers, but the gear information is useful for anyone. It also provides a resource for materials and patterns to make your own gear.

www.ultralight-hiking.com: Gear reviews, sample packing list, and lightweight hiking information.

Gear

While many companies have jumped on the light-weight bandwagon, mainstream manufactured gear is still generally on the heavier end of the spectrum. The following companies either specialize in lightweight gear or have a significant number of products that fall into the lightweight category. In the case of larger manufacturers, I have listed gear categories that fall within lightweight parameters, and which have been reviewed and used by hikers in the lightweight community. These companies also offer a wide range of other gear, some of which may be appropriate for lightweight hiking and some of which is not. Please note that this is not a complete list, and many of the companies that specialize in ultralight equipment are small-scale operations that do most of their business over the Internet. The following information is current as of publication.

www.biblertents.com: Single-wall tents, especially appropriate for mountaineering.
www.BlackDiamondEquipment.com: Offers lightweight tents, in addition to traditional climbing gear.
www.brasslite.com: Sturdy, lightweight, alcohol-burning stoves made of brass.
www.exped.com: Sleeping bags and tents.
www.fanaticfringe.com: Ultralight outdoor gear.
www.FeatheredFriends.com: Specializes in sleeping bags, including some of the lightest on the market, as well as down vests.
www.FroggToggs.com: Inexpensive, water-proof, breathable raingear.
www.golite.com: Offers a wide range of lightweight gear for hiking, climbing, and other outdoor sports; many of the designs are based on Ray Jardine's principles.
www.granitegear.com: Offers lightweight packs, in addition to a traditional line of gear.
www.GVPgear.com: Operated by an extreme ultralight hiker, gear includes packs, trekking poles, and flashlights, as well as how-to information and links.
www.hennessyhammock.com: Lightweight hammock systems.
www.hikelight.com: A variety of lightweight gear.
www.Hilleberg.com: Lightweight tents.
www.IntegralDesigns.com: Lightweight jackets, tents, and bivvies.
www.kelty.com: An old name in mainstream outdoor equipment, Kelty also offers several products for lightweight hikers, including modular, lightweight backpacks and sleeping bags.
www.lightloadtowels.com: Reusable towels that weigh less than half an ounce.
www.lwgear.com: A variety of "one-pound" gear, including packs, tarps, and sleeping blankets.

www.MandatoryGear.com: Ultralight tents, clothing, and dry sacks for adventure racers.

www.Marmot.com: While not specifically a lightweight manufacturer, many of Marmot's high-end, well-made products are extremely lightweight, especially sleeping bags and jackets.

www.moonbowgear.com: Unique designs for ultralight gear, including custom-made, integrated backpacking systems; use your designs, theirs, or a combination.

www.moonstone.com: Sleeping bags and jackets.

www.moosiinerr.com: Variety of camping equipment, including a large selection of Trangia alcohol stoves.

www.Mountainsmith.com: Lightweight sleeping bags and packs, in addition to traditional gear.

www.msrcorp.com: MSR's popular stoves are reliable, but not especially lightweight; some of their tents and carbon trekking poles, however, will be of interest to lightweight hikers.

www.nunatakusa.com: Down-filled outerwear and sleep systems.

www.ospreypacks.com: Lightweight packs, as well as more traditional gear.

www.photonlight.com: Flashlights.

www.prolitegear.com: Internet retailer of standard and lightweight gear.

www.SierraDesigns.com: Their Clip Flashlight tent is a lightweight classic; they also make lightweight jackets.

www.sixmoondesigns.com: Tents and packs.

www.snowpeak.com: Stoves, cooking gear, tarps, and titanium tent pegs.

www.speerhammocks.com: Lightweight hammock systems.

www.suuntousa.com: Makers of compasses and primus stoves.

www.tarptent.com: Lightweight tarp-tents.

www.trailquest.net: Homemade lightweight gear.

www.ula-equipment.com: Custom-made, lightweight backpacks.

www.ursack.com: Bear-resistant stuff sacks.

www.wanderlustgear.com: Lightweight tents.

www.warmlite.com: Tents, sleeping bags, and vapor barrier clothing.

www.westernmountaineering.com: Lightweight, down sleeping bags and vests.

Index

About the Author

Having carried packs ranging from 15 to 85 pounds over six continents, 17,000 miles, and more mountains than she can count, author Karen Berger knows the value of a light pack from first-hand experience. She is one of the few people to have hiked all of America's "triple crown" trails—the Appalachian, Pacific Crest, and Continental Divide Trails—and has been a contributing editor for *Backpacker,* the outdoor expert for GORP.com, the "Outdoor Smarts" columnist for *Scouting,* and a technical consultant for public television's "Trailside." Her magazine articles have appeared in a wide range of publications, including *National Geographic Traveler, Islands, Men's Fitness,* and *Family Circle.* Karen is also the author of nine books, most recently *More Everyday Wisdom: Trail-tested Advice from the Experts* (The Mountaineers Books, 2002). She lives in the Berkshire Hills of southern Massachusetts near the Appalachian Trail. You can check out her latest adventures on her website at www.hikerwriter.com.

THE MOUNTAINEERS, founded in 1906, is a nonprofit outdoor activity and conservation club with 14,000 members, whose mission is "to explore, study, preserve, and enjoy the natural beauty of the outdoors. . . ." The club sponsors many classes and year-round outdoor activities in the Pacific Northwest, and supports environmental causes through educational activities, sponsoring legislation and presenting educational programs. The Mountaineers Books supports the club's mission by publishing travel and natural history guides, instructional texts, and works on conservation and history.

Send or call for our catalog of more than 500 outdoor titles:

The Mountaineers Books
1001 SW Klickitat Way, Suite 201
Seattle, WA 98134
800-553-4453
mbooks@mountaineersbooks.org
www.mountaineersbooks.org

33 East Minor Street
Emmaus, PA 18098
800-666-3434
www.backpacker.com

The mission of *Backpacker* magazine is to provide accurate, useful, in-depth, and engaging information about wilderness recreation in North America.

The Mountaineers Books is proud to be a corporate sponsor of Leave No Trace, whose mission is to promote and inspire responsible outdoor recreation through education, research, and partnerships. The Leave No Trace program is focused specifically on human-powered (nonmotorized) recreation.

Leave No Trace strives to educate visitors about the nature of their recreational impacts, as well as offer techniques to prevent and minimize such impacts. Leave No Trace is best understood as an educational and ethical program, not as a set of rules and regulations.

For more information, visit *www.LNT.org,* or call 800-332-4100.

MORE TITLES IN THE BACKPACKER MAGAZINE SERIES FROM THE MOUNTAINEERS BOOKS

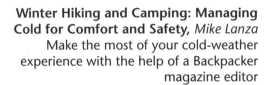

Trekker's Handbook: Strategies to Enhance Your Journey, *Buck Tilton*
Contains pre-trip, during the trip, and post-trip strategies for long-distance hiking

Winter Hiking and Camping: Managing Cold for Comfort and Safety, *Mike Lanza*
Make the most of your cold-weather experience with the help of a Backpacker magazine editor

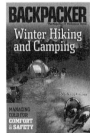

Everyday Wisdom: 1001 Expert Tips for Hikers, *Karen Berger*
Expert tips and tricks for hikers and backpackers selected from one of the most popular *Backpacker* magazine columns

More Everyday Wisdom: Trail-Tested Advice from the Experts, *Karen Berger*
More tips for enhancing backcountry trips

Backcountry Cooking: From Pack to Plate in 10 Minutes, *Dorcas Miller*
Over 144 recipes and how to plan simple meals

More Backcountry Cooking: Moveable Feasts from the Experts, *Dorcas Miller*
Practical, tasty recipes that are quick, easy, and nutritious

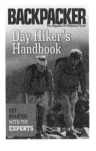

Day Hiker's Handbook: Get Started with the Experts, *Mike Lanza*
Learn how to get started, what gear to choose, and how to handle possible dangers

---

Available at fine bookstores and outdoor stores, by phone at 800-553-4453 or on the web at *www.mountaineersbooks.org*

THE MOUNTAINEERS BOOKS